Lightning Path
Workbook Two

Introduction to the Lightning Path

A Totally New and Different Foundation

Version 1.0

By Michael Sharp

www.michaelsharp.org

Full Divine

I write a poem to share with you,
In hopes this message will get through,
In hopes an arrow for to find,
A heart that's pumping FULL DIVINE.

And if it's not, well sad to say,
I shrug my shoulders in this way,
And say "no skin off my big nose,"
If you decide to curl your toes.

But listen to these words I pray,
The old world it will go away,
And at end of time you're sure to find.
No platform for your graced behind.

So heed this poem, for here I say,
I've come to show a better way,
To make you pause and heed this day.
Please listen, lest the piper plays.

For time is now, just as we planned,
The place is earth, it has God's brand,
Before you know it, told you so.
We'll have a big utopian show.

And if you want to join the fun,
Well listen up, I'm almost done.
The secret's simple, truth so fine,
Just pump your heart out, FULL DIVINE.

Copyright Michael Sharp
www.michaelsharp.org

The technique of mysticism, properly practiced, may result in the direct intuition of and union with an ultimate spiritual reality that is perceived as simultaneously beyond the self and, in some way, within it.
Aldous Huxley

Lightning Path
Workbook Two

Introduction to the Lightning Path

Version 1.0

By Michael Sharp
www.michaelsharp.org

The Lightning Path
www.thelightningpath.com

Published by Lightning Path Press
St. Albert, Alberta Canada
press.thelightningpath.com

©2016 The Lightning Path.
All rights reserved.

No part of this book may be reproduced,
stored in a retrieval system, or transmitted by any means,
electronic, mechanical, photocopying, recording,
or otherwise without written permission.

ISBN Print: 978-1-897455-23-4
ISBN Ebook: 978-1-897455-27-2

Table of Contents

- Preface 8
- Unit Goals 9
- The Lightning Path in a Nutshell 10
- Doubt, Disbelief, and Disappointment 33
- Reconnecting with The Fabric 46
- Origins 71
- Some Challenges 102
- LP Exploration and Exposition Principles 135
- Conclusion: How Long Will it Take? 152
- Organizing Your Workgroup 159
- Key Concepts 161
- Study Questions 163
- About the Author 167
- About the Lightning Path 169
- Index 171
- References 173

Preface

Greetings and welcome to the Lightning Path (or just LP for short). The Lightning Path is a powerful, effective, grounded, logical, intuitive, modern, and authentic path of spiritual awakening, activation, and ascension. The Lightning Path is the child of Dr. Michael S., a university professor in Sociology, counselor, and practicing mystic. It has been in development for over a decade and is designed to provide a rapid path toward authentic spiritual experience and personal rediscovery of deep spiritual truths unencumbered by oppressive structures, greed, corruption, profiteering, and ego. The Lightning Path is a proposed solution to the economic and ecological crises identified and discussed in *Rocket Scientists' Guide to Money and the Economy: Accumulation and Debt*.[1]

The workbook that you have in your hands right now is the introduction to the Lightning Path itself. This book provides you with information about the Lightning Path and includes a discussion of the origins, principles, purpose, and goals of LP spirituality. Because this book deals with the Lightning Path itself and not actual spiritual technique, you may be tempted to skip. Please don't. If you do, you will miss key grounding information that you may need later. If you skip these lessons and find you are struggling with concepts, information, practice, or outcomes, return to these lessons and complete them as guided.

---

[1] Michael Sharp, The Rocket Scientists' Guide to Money and the Economy: Accumulation and Debt. (St Albert, Alberta: Lightning Path Press., 2016).

Unit Goals

By the end of this introductory booklet you should:

1. Have a clear understanding of the nature, scope, and origins of the Lightning Path.

2. Have a feel for where the Lightning Path might fit in your own belief system and/or spiritual aspirations.

3. Understand some of the challenges that we all face when dealing with the, arguably, infiltrated and corrupt spirituality of this planet.

4. Understand the principles which form the foundations upon which Lightning Path is developed.

The Lightning Path in a Nutshell

Greetings and welcome to The Lightning Path (or just LP for short). The Lightning Path is a powerful, effective, grounded, logical, intuitive, modern, and authentic path of spiritual awakening, activation, and ascension. The Lightning Path is designed to provide a path toward personal rediscovery of deep spiritual truths, unencumbered by oppressive social structures, greed, corruption, profiteering, and **Bodily Ego**.[2] Put in LP terms, the Lightning Path is designed to get you connected with what I call the **Fabric of Consciousness**[3] (or just The Fabric for short). The LP is designed to put you in touch with the inner core of your divinity and to get you experiencing the high spiritual truths of creation for yourself. The goal of the Lightning Path is nothing more nor less than your growth and maturation into the spark of divine consciousness that you really and truly are.

Connection

Now, this might seem like a little thing stated in this fashion, maybe even a delusional thing, but it is not. Getting you reconnected to your spark of Divine Consciousness is, in my opinion, the biggest and best thing that you will ever do in this life, or in any life for that matter. Indeed, **Connection**[4] with The Fabric of Consciousness is the ultimate goal of all **authentic**

---

[2] The bodily ego is the ego of your physical body. The bodily ego is distinct and separate from your spiritual ego. For more, see http://www.thespiritwiki.com/Bodily_Ego and http://www.thespiritwiki.com/Spiritual_Ego

[3] The Fabric of Consciousness is the underlying substrate of reality. It is what Semites call Aun and what Hindus call Brahman. This is a very important LP concept. For more, see http://www.thespiritwiki.com/Fabric_of_Consciousness.

[4] Connection is the Lightning Path term for what occurs when the Bodily Ego of the Physical Unit unites with your higher Self (i.e. your **Resident Monadic Consciousness**) or some higher level of the Fabric of Consciousness. For more, see http://www.thespiritwiki.com/Connection and http://www.thespiritwiki.com/Resident_Monadic_Consciousness

spirituality.[5] Whether you realize it yet or not, the deeper purpose and uncorrupted intent of all major spiritual traditions (whether these traditions be esoteric or exoteric) is reconnection with the Divine. As the famous American psychologist William James said, "All major religious and spiritual traditions are built on the mystical experience of specialized pattern-setters."[6] Another American psychologist, Abraham Maslow, echoed James when he said:

> The very beginning, the intrinsic core, the essence, the universal nucleus of every known high religion... has been the private, lonely, personal illumination, revelation, or ecstasy of some acutely sensitive prophet or seer. The high religions call themselves revealed religions and *each of them tends to rest its validity, its function, and its right to exist on the codification and the communication of this original mystic experience* or revelation from the lonely prophet to the mass of human beings in general.[7]

As both James and Maslow recognized, the "pattern setters" have all said the same thing and have all pointed to the same goal, which is reconnection to the divine spark of Consciousness that lies deeply submerged and occluded within you.

At first glance suggesting that reconnection (or just simply connection) is the purpose and the point of **authentic spirituality**[8] might seem like a very unusual thing to suggest, but

---

[5] Authentic spirituality is spirituality that connects. Authentic spirituality is spirituality that provides archetypes, concepts, guidance, and training that leads to authentic and real Connection with The Fabric of Consciousness.

For more, see the SpiritWiki entry at www.thespiritwiki.com/Authentic_Spirituality and Michael Sharp, The Rocket Scientists' Guide to Authentic Spirituality (St. Albert, Alberta: Lightning Path Press, 2010).

Also see http://www.thespiritwiki.com/Authentic_Spirituality.

[6] William James, The Varieties of Religious Experience: A Study of Human Nature (New York: Penguin, 1982) 6.

[7] A. H. Maslow, "The "Core-Religious" or "Transcendent" Experience," The Highest State of Consciousness, ed. John White (New York: Doubleday, 2012) 339.emphasis added

[8] Authentic spirituality is spirituality that helps you connect.

it is not. Indeed, you don't have to go very deep into mystical/religious traditions of this planet to see that connection to The Fabric (i.e. connection to God) is the ubiquitous desiderata and **Holy Grail**[9] of mystical experience. Western mystics talk about the experiences of gnosis,[10] oneness, connection with the incorruptible one,[11] or the descent of Christ consciousness. Getting reconnected is what Hindus call *Samādhi,*[12] *Sat-Chit-Ananda,* or the boundless bliss of Brahman. It is what Sufis call *Fana,*[13] and what Buddhists call *Satori.*[14] In the Tibetan Book of the Dead we connect to the *Clear Light.*[15] Evangelical Christians speak of being "born again" into that Light. Mystical Christians call the Fabric the *Living Flame of Love,*[16] the *Love-Fire,*[17] and call reconnection the experience of *Inward Light.*[18] And it is not just in our big religious/spiritual traditions that we find this. Scientologists refer to the outcome of connection as being "clear" and pagan and indigenous religions have long traditions of encouraging *shamanic experiences*[19] (i.e. reconnection experiences), often

---

[9] The Holy Grail is a spiritual metaphor for full and empowered Connection. The Holy Grail is a cup filled with the glorious wine of Consciousness. See http://www.thespiritwiki.com/Holy_Grail

[10] Rev. W. R. Inge, Mysticism in Religion (New York: Hutchinson's University Library, 2005) 9. Gnosis is "not merely hearsay and dependence" on the teachings of others. Gnosis is that "which envisages the unseen for itself. For it does not believe on a person, it believes in and into him." In other words, gnosis is direct mystical experience that you yourself have.

[11] Frederik Wisse, "The Apocryphon of John," The Nag Hammadi Library (New York: Harper Collins, 1990) 105. John the mystic accounts a powerful mystical experience where he speaks directly to the "incorruptible one" on the nature of consciousness, creation, and emanation.

[12] H. Zimmer, Philosophies of India (Princeton, NJ: University Press, 1951).

[13] Llewellyn Vaughan-Lee, Catching the Thread: Sufism, Dreamwork & Jungian Psychology (Inverness, CA: Golden Sufi Center, 1998).

[14] H. Smith, The Religions of Man (New York: Harper & Row, 1958).

[15] W.Y. Evans-Wents, The Tibetan Book of the Dead, or the after-Death Experiences of the Bardo Plane, According to Lama Kazi Dawa-Samdup's English Rendering [1927] (London: Oxford University Press, 1960).

[16] John of the Cross, The Living Flame of Love, trans. Ackerman J (Kindle: Magisterium Press, 2015).

[17] J. Boehme, The Signature of All Things, with Other Writings (London: J.M. Dent & Sons, 1912).

[18] T.R. Kelly, A Testament of Devotion (New York: Harper & Brothers, 1941).

[19] M. Eliade, Shamanism: Archaic Techniques of Ecstasy (New York: Pantheon Books, 1964).

with the assistance of entheogenic substances.

Notably, it is not just the mystically and spiritually inclined who speak of connection to the Fabric. Philosophers, scientists, and scholars talk about it as well. Plato referred to it in his allegory of the cave and noted that it wasn't the shadows on the screen (i.e. the reality in front of your eyes right now) that was real, it was the Reality (with a capital "R") that was behind you (i.e. within you) where the Truth lay.[20] Dionysius the Greek said it was all about "incomprehensible union with Him"[21] and R. Otto said we touched the *Numinous*.[22] R.W.R. Inge (1860-1954), an Anglican priest and professor of divinity at Cambridge, writes:

> [It] means communion with God. That is to say with a Being conceived as the supreme and ultimate reality. If what the mystics say of their experience is true, if they have really been in communion with the Holy Spirit of God, that is a fact of overwhelming importance which must be taken into account when we attempt to understand God, the world, and ourselves."[23]

Evelyn Underhill said that a mystical experience is a reconnection experience[24] (I would say **Connection Experience**)[25] and said that we reconnect with Reality (with a capital "R").[26] Bucke, a Canadian medical doctor, calls it *Cosmic*

---

[20] Plato, The Republic (New York: Dover Publications, 2000).

[21] A. Vergote, "Plying between Psychology and Mysticism," Mysticism: A Variety of Psychological Perspectives, eds. Jacob A Belzen and Antoon Geels (New York: Rodopi, 2003) 81.

[22] Rudolf Otto, The Idea of the Holy (Oxford: Oxford University Press, 1917).

[23] Inge, Mysticism in Religion 8.

[24] Evelyn Underhill, Mysticism: A Study in the Nature and Development of Spiritual Consciousness (New York: Dover Publications, 2002 (1911)) 81.

[25] A connection experience is the LP term for mystical/spiritual experience. We use the term "connection" because a mystical experience is a connection between your body/mind, and higher Consciousness. For more see http://www.thespiritwiki.com/Connection_Experience

[26] Underhill, Mysticism: A Study in the Nature and Development of Spiritual Consciousness.

Consciousness.[27] Happold says Ultimate Reality.[28] F.W.H. Myers says *Subliminal Consciousness.*[29] Psychologists get in on the act, describing connection with God as a transcendent or peak experience.[30] You can even find engineers waxing poetic. Robert G. Jahn, former dean of engineering at Princeton University and psychologist Brenda Dunne call it The Source and went on to say:

> [W]e reject the popular presumption that all modes of human information processing are completely executed within the physiological brain, and that all experiential sensations are epiphenomena of the biophysical and biochemical states thereof. Rather, we ... regard the brain as a neurologically localized utility that serves a much more extended "mind," or "psyche," or "consciousness" that far transcends the brain in its capacity, range, endurance, and subtlety of operation, and that is far more sophisticated than a mere antenna for information acquisition or a silo for its storage. In fact, we ... contend that it [extended mind, psyche, consciousness] is the ultimate organizing principle of the universe, creating reality through its ongoing dialogue with the unstructured potentiality of the Source. In short, we subscribe to the assertion of [astrophysicist] Arthur Eddington nearly a century ago: "Not once in the dim past, but continuously, by conscious mind is the miracle of the Creation wrought."[31]

Beyond the statements of the diehard mystics and scientists, we

---

[27] R.M. Bucke, Cosmic Consciousness (New York: E.P. Dutton, 2009/1929), Edward. Carpenter, The Art of Creation: Essays on the Self and Its Powers (London: Georbe Allen & Unwin, 1921).

[28] F.C. Happold, Mysticism: A Study and Anthology (New York: Penguin Books, 1963).

[29] F.W.H. Myers, "The Subliminal Consciousness," Proc Soc Psychical Res 7 (1892).

[30] See for example A. H. Maslow, Religions, Values, and Peak-Experiences (New York: Penguin, 1994). Also A.H. Maslow, The Farther Reaches of Human Nature (New York: Viking, 1971). A.H. Maslow, "A Theory of Human Motivation," Psychological Review 50.4 (1943)..

[31] R. Jahn and B. Dunne, "Sensors, Filters, and the Source of Reality," Filters and Reflections: Perspectives on Reality, eds. Z. Jones, B. Dunne, E. Hoeger and R. Jahn (Princeton: ICRL Press, 2009) 3-4.

also find notions of the Fabric and connection peppered throughout the music and art of this planet. Indeed, we find mystical connection and mystical experience to be a common desiderata and a ubiquitous "thing" in the music, art, literature, and drama of this planet. Dante called it Universal Form.[32] Author William Blake called "it" Imaginative Vision.[33] Bob Marley speaks about Exodus and connection with Jah (God). Fat Boy Slim speaks about shelter and authenticity.[34] Arthur C. Clarke, in his novel *Childhood's End,* wrote about an evolving connection to *Overmind.*[35] Both the *Divine Comedy* by Dante and *Paradise Lost* by Milton attempt to represent this connection in literary form. As one commentator on Dante and Milton points out, mystical experience, mystical reconnection, or *coming face to face with God,* is nothing less than *redemption.*

> One of the most striking matters in *The Divine Comedy* and *Paradise Lost* is the vision of God. Both poet's chief concern is with the redemption of man [sic] and this is possible only after the realization of God...though Dante was Catholic and Milton Protestant, at the end of The Divine Comedy and Paradise Lost, both Catholic and Protestant philosophies seem to converge and we find both poets face to face with the self-same God. All sorts of differences seem to vanish. There is no place for duality after the vision of God.[36]

Finally, one of the most brilliant pieces of Western Classical music, Beethoven's *Ninth Symphony,* and in particular his final movement *Ode to Joy,* is a joyful hymn to reconnection. Despite the cultural confusion surrounding the piece, to the

---

[32] Dante Alighieri, The Divine Comedy, trans. Henry Johnson (New Haven: Yale University Press, 1915). Canto 33, line 91

[33] William Blake, The Portable Blake (New York: Penguin, 1977).

[34] See "Song for Shelter" by Fatboy Slim. 934

[35] Arthur C Clarke, Childhood's End (New York: Del Rey, 1987).

[36] Hitesh Parmar, Paradise Lost and the Divine Comedy: A Comparative Study (New Delhi: Sarup & Sons, 2002) 129.

"initiated" (i.e. one who has had a connection experience or two) the meaning is clear. The words Beethoven chose speak of triumphant reconnection in terms that any mystic would find meaningful and true. We enter the "heavenly sanctuary" as passionately burning "spark[s] of divinity."

> Joy, beautiful spark of divinity,
> Daughter from Elysium,
> We enter, burning with fervour,
> heavenly being, your sanctuary!
> Your magic brings together
> what fashion has sternly divided.
> All men shall become brothers,
> Wherever your gentle wings hover.

Notably, the outcome of this reconnection is the collapse of separation. When we reconnect, the magic will reunite us all in a glorious "brotherhood"[37] of love and life.

Beethoven chose Friedrich Schiller's *Ode to Joy* poem as the lyrical basis of the fourth movement, and while I do not agree with the patriarchy of the poem (women are not mentioned in the bliss of reunion that accompanies connection with "Him"), nor do I support Schiller's portrayal of the Fabric as a "loving father", nevertheless the *Ode to Joy* is the most brilliant and triumphant hymn to the powerful joy/bliss of reconnection that has ever been expressed. No individual on the planet even comes close to Beethoven's awe inspiring hosanna to reconnection with the Fabric.

As you can see, connection (or reconnection, depending on how you want to look at it) is a big deal. *Connection is salvation, pure and simple.* Indeed, reconnection is nothing more nor less

---

[37] Sexist language alert.

than the actual experience of the Kingdom of Heaven/God. Whatever it is called, it refers to the same thing. The purpose and the point of all authentic spirituality is to reconnect with the Fabric of Consciousness, to experience and live The Kingdom. And it is the same with the Lightning Path. The goal of the Lightning Path, like the ostensible (if not always actualized) goal of every major spiritual system on this planet, is mystical connection to the Fabric of Consciousness. The Fabric of Consciousness, which is described in volume one of my *Book of Light,* is Ultimate Reality, Universal Form, Buddha Mind, Para Brahman, pure Consciousness, or God by any other name. The Fabric of Consciousness is what mystics and others connect to when they have their mystical/peak experiences. On the Lightning Path, we say that *a mystical experience occurs when you reconnect (even if only temporarily) with the Fabric of Consciousness*

Spiritual Emancipation

If I've tweaked your interest a bit and you are still reading, great. If you can accept for the moment that there might be something in mystical experience worth talking about, and if you can control the programmed and dogmatic rejection that sometimes occurs when this topic is broached, the next question we want to address is "Why?"

Why bother with something like that?

Why strive toward mystical experience?

Why drive yourself toward the bliss of Brahman?

Why look to be born again?

Why seek reconnection with The Fabric?

Well, I can tell you that you don't do this just so you can please some big beard wearing patriarch in the sky. It is not about following commandments, pleasing daddy, or worshipping the "Big Guy." All that stuff has nothing to do with authentic connection experience. To be blunt, all that stuff is merely authoritarian propaganda designed to get you to embrace the slavery of **The System**[38] by encouraging you to willingly give up your freedom to the closest authority figure around you. If you want the truth, you reconnect, i.e. you look to be "born again," *so you can break the materialist chains that bind you.*[39] If you want the truth, you look to reconnect so you can *remember, recognize, and embrace your true divine self.* If I was to lay it all on the line, you connect so you can be who you truly are! And that is a good thing because who you truly are is a lot bigger than what you have been taught (I would say indoctrinated) to believe.

It is true.

You have been indoctrinated to believe that you are a fallen soul, an evolving ape, or some hopeless (and sometimes worthless and dirty[40]) little cosmic school child in need of lifetimes of karmic instruction. You have been told that you are cosmic dust in the wind. You have been told that you are here for a good time, but gone for a long time. But as any mystic will tell you, you are a lot bigger than all that, and that is the point of mystical experience. The point of reconnecting with The Fabric and having mystical experiences is so you can realize who you really are and embrace your true **Self**.[41] This is the

---

[38] For an introduction to The System, see Sharp, The Rocket Scientists' Guide to Money and the Economy: Accumulation and Debt. Also see http://www.thespiritwiki.com/The_System

[39] The authentic spiritual goal of spiritual emancipation is expressed in the Halo/Sharp Emancipation card from my own Halo/Sharp Archetype/Tarot deck. This card shows human hands breaking the spiritual chains of The System, chains that bind us in delusion, Maya, and materialist slavery.

For some background on the modern tarot you can see Mike Sosteric, "A Sociology of Tarot," Canadian Journal of Sociology 39.3 (2014). For a more detailed explication of the Halo/Sharp tarot, and its fundamental break with the Masonic Rider-Waite deck (which is, as I note in my article *The Sociology of Tarot,* an elite deck inscribed with elite interests), see the three volumes of my *Book of the Triumph of Spirit* series. Michael Sharp, The Book of the Triumph of Spirit: Master Key (St Albert, Alberta: Lightning Path Press, Unpublished), Michael Sharp, The Book of Triumph of Spirit: Healing and Activating with the Halo/Sharp System (St. Albert: Lightning Path Press, 2013), Michael Sharp, The Book of the Triumph of Spirit: Halo/Sharp New Energy Archetypes, St. Albert.

[40] It might sound strange to some with no experience of religious indoctrination, but I was told by my Catholic indoctrinators that I was a dirty little cosmic turdball.

[41] The term Self with a capital "S" refers to your "higher self" or Resident Monadic Consciousness in LP

point of spiritual practice and the Holy Grail of authentic spirituality. When mystical connection occurs, when you reach in and touch the divine spark that is within you, you are *freed* (more or less) from the slavery of material existence (the bondage of Egypt as it is sometimes put) and the delusions of Maya.[42] Put in the nomenclature of the Lightning Path, having authentic mystical experiences *emancipates you*[43] from the bondage of The System.

Making the mystical connection and experiencing emancipation, even if it is only very brief, is a wonderful gift! As mystics, writers, musicians, and others have pointed out over the centuries, and as I (as one who has experienced the connection many times can attest), there isn't anything more joyful than the full realization of the divine glory buried deep inside you, and there isn't anything more satisfying and fulfilling than the emancipatory personal transformation that this brings for you. Not even the slickest, most expensive, most technologically advanced Hollywood experience even comes close to the power, the glory, and the bliss of the transformation wrought by authentic reconnection with the Fabric of Consciousness. And I'm not the only one to say this. Abraham Maslow, a pioneer of Humanistic psychology waxes proximally to poetic expression when speaking of his study and analysis of peak experiences. Speaking of healthy people who have mystical experience he says...

> I learned many lessons from these people. But one in particular is our concern now. I found that these

---

nomenclature. The term self with a small "s" refers, in LP nomenclature, to your bodily ego. See http://www.thespiritwiki.com/Self

[42] http://en.wikipedia.org/wiki/Maya_(illusion)

[43] I say "potentially" here because even a powerful mystical experience can amount to nothing if you turn away from it or forget you ever had it. This is more often the case than you might imagine. Many children have mystical experiences of a very deep and profound nature, however because our society is setup the way it is, because authentic mystical experiences are often resisted and even denied by others, children don't talk and eventually forget. It is the same with adults. Despite the fact that most adults report having mystical experiences of one sort or another, most adults never talk about it, never explore the implications, and never think to encourage a wider and deeper connection. As a result of the resistance and denial, they eventually forget and when they do, they return to "normal" consciousness and "normal" life as if nothing significant ever happened at all.

individuals tended to report having had something like mystic experiences, moments of great awe, moments of the most intense happiness or even rapture, ecstacy [sic] or bliss (because the word happiness can be too weak to describe this experience).

These moments were of pure, positive happiness when all doubts, all fears, all inhibitions, all tensions, all weaknesses, were left behind. Now self consciousness was lost. All separateness and distance from the world disappeared as they felt one with the world, fused with it, really belonging in it and to it, instead of being outside looking in. (One subject said, for instance, "I felt like a member of a family, not like an orphan.").

Perhaps most important of all, however, was the report in these experiences of the feeling that they had really seen the ultimate truth, the essence of things, the secret of life, as if veils had been pulled aside. Alan Watts has described this feeling as, "This is it!" as if you had finally gotten there, as if ordinary life was a striving and a straining to get someplace and this was the arrival, this was Being There!: the end of straining and of striving, the achievement of the desire and the hope, the fulfillment of the longing and the yearning. Everyone knows how it feels to want something and not know what. These mystic experiences feel like the ultimate satisfaction of vague, unsatisfied stepping into heaven; like the miracle achieved, like perfection finally attained."

And note, it is not just spiritual emancipation, realization of our fundamental divinity, pure bliss/rapture/ecstasy, awe, wonder, glory, and deep satisfaction that is at stake here. Remembering and embracing who you are is great, but what happens to your world (to the world) when you reconnect is even better. With reconnection to The Fabric, you can generally look forward to increased self-knowledge, increased mental health, increased

---

" A. H. Maslow, "Lessons from the Peak-Experiences," Journal of Humanistic Psychology 2.1 (1962): 8-9.

empowerment, renewed understanding, enhanced wisdom, deeper insight, the development of an advanced moral sensibility, sharpened intellectual functioning, enhancements in artistic capability, and more. Psychologists as early as William James[45] and Abraham Maslow believed in the positive efficacy of peak experiences,[46] but the last ten years of scientific research has demonstrated not only the validity of mystical experiences[47] but their salutatory effect on mental and emotional health as well.[48] I would even argue, in fact I have argued in my *Rocket Scientists' Guide to Money and the Economy*,[49] that authentic mystical connection leads to personal empowerment, global unity, and planetary transformation! Indeed, someone who has had authentic spiritual experiences engages in life in a much different way than someone who has not. Someone who has had authentic mystical experiences engages in life as the powerful *creator* they really are.

As you can see, there really are a lot of good reasons to move forward with your study and practice. If you want my advice, starting right here, right now, you should strive toward mystical reconnection with The Fabric because nothing, and when I say nothing I mean nothing, will ever bring your life more meaning and purpose, more fulfillment and joy, than following an authentic path toward authentic reconnection with the glorious Fabric of Consciousness.

---

[45] James, The Varieties of Religious Experience: A Study of Human Nature.

[46] Maslow, Religions, Values, and Peak-Experiences, A. H. Maslow, Motivation and Personality (2nd Ed.) (New York: Harper & Row, 1970), Maslow, The Farther Reaches of Human Nature, A. H. Maslow, Towards a Psychology of Being (2nd Edition) (New York: Van Nostrand Reinhold Company, 1968), Maslow, "Lessons from the Peak-Experiences."

[47] Andrew Newberg and Mark Robert Waldman, How God Changes Your Brain: Breakthrough Findings from a Leading Neuroscientist (New York: Ballantine Books, 2009), Andew Newberg, Eugene d'Aquile and Vince Rause, Why God Won't Go Away: Brain Science and the Biology of Belief, ed. New York (New York: Ballantine Books, 2001).,

[48] George Drazenovich and Celia Kourie, "Mysticismand Mental Health: Acritical Dialogue," Hervormde Teologiese Studies 66.2 (2010), C. C. H. Cook, "Psychiatry and Mysticism," Mental Health, Religion & Culture 7.2 (2004).

[49] Sharp, The Rocket Scientists' Guide to Money and the Economy: Accumulation and Debt.

Getting Connected

At this point you know that the Lightning Path is about facilitating mystical connection, you know a bit about what the mystical connection entails, you know that mystical connection is a common subject and universal desiderata, and you have some positive statements about the utility and benefit of mystical connection to The Fabric of Consciousness. If you are still interested in the phenomenon of mystical reconnection, and if I have gotten you interested in striving toward this "union of unions," the next question becomes how do you facilitate reconnection?

How do you get to experience the bliss of Brahman?

How do you become enlightened?

How do you attain satori?

How do you get clear?

How do you become born again?

How do you get back to **The Garden**?[50]

How do you enter the **Kingdom of God**?[51]

Answering the question of how to reconnect brings us back to the Lightning Path. As I said earlier, *the LP is designed to help you reconnect.* As you will discover in more detail as you progress, the LP does this by

a) providing clear concepts and precise, unambiguous information,

b) modernizing the core spiritual teachings,

c) removing corruption and ideology (i.e. purifying the Truth),

d) pointing in the general direction of mental, emotional,

---

[50] The phrase The Garden refers to a condition of existence characterized by collective alignment with Consciousness. For more see http://www.thespiritwiki.com/The_Garden

[51] The Kingdom of God is just another way of saying The Garden.

and physical healing, and

e) providing a safe and proper foundation for mystical advancement.

Now, perhaps this does not sound like much at this point, especially if you have never had a full blown mystical connection. However, if you have "blown open the doors of perception," if you have "kissed the sky" and been burned by the light, if you have been scared and scarred to the point of traumatic shutdown, if you have descended into pre-psychotic or even psychotic madness as the result of a bad trip, if life trauma or anxiety has ever tipped you over the deep end, or if some "not-so-nice-person" has exploited your spiritual/mystical naiveté and openness in order to spin you down a dark hallway and turn you around in circles, you will know what I'm talking about here, and you will understand the need for training. It is one thing to go to church and kneel before your God or to worship at the foot of a guru; it is quite another to pursue authentic mystical connection with the Fabric of Consciousness under your own intent and authority. The former (i.e. spiritual submission to authority) is a game that frightened children and confused adults play. The latter is what people seeking to grow up into powerful, spiritually attuned adults seek to do. The latter is what the LP assists you to do.

Staying Connected

Of course, getting you connected is not the whole ball of wax. The Lightning Path provides guidance on how to get connected, that is true; but the LP also provides you with the guidance and support you need to <u>stay connected</u>, and staying connected is really the central issue! As you will learn as you progress through the teachings, it is one thing to have a brief connection experience or two, it is one thing to experience the glory and unity of consciousness for a moment, it is one thing to get a **glimpse**[52] of The Kingdom, but it is quite another to be permanently enlightened, uplifted, and transformed by it. The problem is that the experience often does not stick. The problem is, people see The Kingdom but turn their back on the gate. The problem is, people often have an experience or two, but settle back down into a lifetime of "normal" again.

Why?

For various reasons, some of which I can mention here, but none of which I will go into detail about. **For one,** *we can have a hard time coping with the power of experience.* The Fabric of Consciousness is powerful, grand, and glorious and as many mystics have pointed out, its experience can be engulfing and overwhelming. The power of the experience can sometimes be too much for unprepared and/or damaged minds (see below) to cope with, ground, and integrate. If we are not prepared, or if we lose our footing, we can temporarily blow a fuse or even permanently short a circuit. When this happens, fear, anxiety, and discombobulation can cause us to back away or even flee the spiritual arena. In some cases, the experience can be so overwhelming, and the fear and even paranoia that arises as a result of the "dark," **old energy**[53] **archetypes**[54] implanted in the brain so great, that individuals sacrifice their potential for connection and never return to spiritual pursuit.

Having a hard time coping with the experience of connection (i.e. having a hard time coping with a full blown mystical experience) is not the only reason we have difficulty staying

---

[52] A glimpse is a sudden, often unexpected, and usually very brief Connection to a higher level of Consciousness than an individual is "normally" used to experiencing. For more, see http://www.thespiritwiki.com/Glimpse

[53] Old Energy is a Lightning Path phrase used to describe energy that is imbalanced (prevalence of yang/force), violent, hierarchical, dominating, exclusionary, elitist, and in the most extreme cases, psychopathic. See http://www.thespiritwiki.com/Old_Energy

[54] An archetype is any conscious or unconscious idea that provides an individual with an answer to a **Big Question**. For example, the image of God as a celestial patriarch is a common Christian archetype that answers the big question, where did we come from.

Big questions are the ultimate questions of our existence, like who are we, why did we come, and what is our purpose. See http://www.thespiritwiki.com/Archetypes and http://www.thespiritwiki.com/Big_Questions

connected. **Another reason** we struggle with connection is because of the violence we experience. It is true that the violence[55] and disregard of this world can pull us back down and break, or even totally prevent, our connection to the Fabric. And I want to emphasize here that this is *not* a mystical process, it is a simple case of damage to the **physical unit**.[56] *Violence of all forms, especially chronic violence at the hands of people you trust, damages the physical unit and prevents connection*, and this is true whether or not damage is the active damage of violence and assault, or the passive damage of disregard and neglect. It is now a well-established fact in the scientific research of this planet that **toxic socialization**[57] experiences, i.e. child abuse, neglect, and even poverty hamper the development of the physical unit and undermine realization of its full potential. The most striking impact is on brain size. As Joan Luby points out, the experience of poverty means *smaller brains!*

> ...exposure to poverty during early childhood is associated with smaller white matter, cortical gray matter, and hippocampal and amygdala volumes measured at school age/early adolescence. These findings extend the substantial body of behavioral data demonstrating the deleterious effects of poverty on child developmental outcomes into the neurodevelopmental domain and are consistent with prior results.[58]

---

[55] When I use the word "violence" I always, unless specified otherwise, have in mind all forms of physical, emotional, psychological, financial, and spiritual violence. For me violence is any act that hurts and undermines the health, autonomy, integrity, and existence of another person.

[56] The phrase physical unit (PU) is the LP term for your physical body *and* brain. The phrase physical unit refers to both your body and the mind/thoughts/bodily ego that emerge out of your physical brain. Put another way, the physical unit is a container/vehicle for incarnated monadic consciousness. See http://www.thespiritwiki.com/Physical_Unit

[57] Toxic Socialization is a socialization process specifically designed to fracture attachments, undermine self-esteem, destroy ego boundaries, and disable the body's ability to contain higher levels of Consciousness. http://www.thespiritwiki.com/Toxic_Socialization. For an overview of the impact of toxic socialization, see Mike Sosteric, "Toxic Socialization," Socjourn (2016).

[58] J. Luby, A. Belden, K. Botteron and et al., "The Effects of Poverty on Childhood Brain Development: The Mediating Effect of Caregiving and Stressful Life Events," JAMA Pediatrics 167.12 (2013).

See also H. Yoshikawa, J. L. Aber and W. R. Beardslee, "The Effects of Poverty on the Mental, Emotional, and

As I noted above mystical experience is powerful. If you are going to be able to cope with it properly, you not only need to be prepared, but your mind has to be healthy and strong. In our world, toxic socialization and perpetual violence, including the perpetual violence of poverty and disregard, undermines the mental and emotional strength of the physical unit and makes it a challenge not just to achieve connection, but to maintain it as well. And note, <u>I am not presenting a hopeless case here</u>. It is possible to heal, develop, and reconnect even for a profoundly damaged physical unit and brain. It just takes a lot of work! Those who come from disadvantaged and/or toxic backgrounds (and note that people who come from wealthy backgrounds can also experience extreme toxicity in their family and social environments) will struggle, and they will need help, support, understanding, and healing in order to advance and stay connected.

The power of the experience and a damaged physical unit can make consistent connection difficult, but other factors interfere with connection as well. **A third factor** is the **blocking emotions**[59] of guilt, shame, fear, paranoia. I won't go into detail about this here except to say that these emotions arise because of the ideas and archetypes that we have in our head. That is, archetypes in our head induce guilt, shame, fear, and paranoia. They do this by pushing us to interpret the experiences in a certain way. For example, archetypes of God as a punishing patriarch push us towards guilt, shame, and anxiety. As you will see when I recount my first **clearing experience**[60] below, archetypes such as

---

Behavioral Health of Children and Youth: Implications for Prevention," <u>Am Psychol</u> 67.4 (2012).

[59] Blocking emotions are emotions, like guilt, shame, fear, paranoia, and anger that cause an individual Physical Unit to block Connection. See http://www.thespiritwiki.com//Blocking_Emotions

[60] A clearing experience is a psychological and/or emotional event whereby an individual successfully clears a **connection blockage** (usually a fear, misconception, or ideologically implanted archetype) that interferes with and/or prevents the physical unit from connecting to a higher level of consciousness. When I told God to f-off, I had a clearing experience. For more see http://www.thespiritwiki.com/Clearing_Experiences and www.thespiritwiki.com/Connection_Blockage

these, which I call **old energy archetypes**,[61] can cause us to flee from higher experiences and our higher Self. This is a problem. The truth is we, and by "we" I mean all humans, have had inserted into our consciousness a series of archetypes and ideas that are designed to support The System and prevent connection. These archetypes are seeded by **Agents of Consciousness**[62] during our socialization and education. These archetypes induce skepticism, misconception, fear, and even paranoia (for example that God is going to punish you for being bad). These old energy archetypes create mental and emotional orientations that make initial and persistent connection to consciousness a challenge. I speak in a lot more detail about archetypes and ideas and their impact on our bodily consciousness in my *Book of the Triumph of Spirit* series, and I also talk about my own experiences overcoming these archetypes below, so here I won't go into any more detail except to say that *old energy archetypes are powerful and pre-emptive; if you are going to advance beyond the most basic levels of spiritual connection, you are going to have to address the old energy archetypes in your consciousness.* The sooner you address and clear old energy archetypes, the easier your connection attempts will be.

It is very true that the power of mystical connection experiences, the damage to our physical unit, and the old energy archetypes which percolate in our consciousness can all make initial and persistent connection difficult. In addition to these, a fourth obstacle to persistent and consistent connection is our own misaligned and toxic behaviors. The reality is, if you engage in bad behaviors, if you act without love, compassion, understanding, strength, courage, and fortitude, you set yourself

---

[61] Old Energy Archetypes are archetypes designed to disconnect the bodily ego from The Fabric of Consciousness. Old Energy archetypes suppress Consciousness and prevent it from descending into the physical unit. http://www.thespiritwiki.com/Old_Energy_Archetypes

[62] An agent of consciousness is an agent of socialization whose specific purpose is to insert ideas and archetypes into the individual and collective consciousness of this planet. See http://www.thespiritwiki.com/Agents_of_Consciousness

out of **alignment**[63] with your higher consciousness, or your **Resident Monadic Self (RMS)**[64] as I call it. Being out of alignment sets you in a state of emotional and psychological **disjuncture**,[65] and this disjuncture causes you to experience powerful negative emotions of guilt, shame, regret, and so on. When your actions are far out of alignment, then the experience of guilt, shame, and other negative emotions can cause you to turn away from your own spiritual connection, and that's a bad thing. If you turn away from connection, you step off the path and go back to normal.

The idea that guilt and shame can cause you to disconnect from your own Resident Monadic Self (RMS) can seem a bit odd, but that is only because you do not understand the psychological and emotional dynamics of your physical unit. As I explain in detail elsewhere,[66] your physical unit is a container or vehicle for a portion of your full **Consciousness**.[67] As a vehicle for Consciousness, your physical body is exactly like an automobile and your consciousness is exactly like the individual who gets in and drives the automobile. The only significant difference between the physical unit your Consciousness drives

---

[63] Alignment is a concept that refers to the state of the physical reality as an accurate and pure reflection of Consciousness. When physical reality accurately reflects the will, intent, and desires of Consciousness we say that physical creation is in alignment with Consciousness. When the physical universe is "off" in some way, we say that physical creation is out of alignment.

The concept of alignment can be difficult to wrap your head around, but for the sake of your own spiritual progress and mental and emotional health, it is critical you understand it. http://www.thespiritwiki.com/Alignment

[64] The Resident Monadic Self is another word for your higher Self or your soul. It is *connection* to this capital "Y" You that is the goal of LP spiritual practice.

[65] Disjuncture is the emotional and psychological stress that arises when the physical unit is out of alignment with its Resident Monadic Consciousness. Disjuncture arises when there is a disconnect between what Consciousness wants and what is actually happening in the material world around you. See http://www.thespiritwiki.com/Disjuncture

[66] Michael Sharp, The Great Awakening: Concepts and Techniques for Successful Spiritual Practice (St. Albert, Alberta, Canada: Lightning Path Press, 2007).

[67] It is impossible to convey a good understanding of Consciousness in a single word, so suffice it to say at this point that Consciousness is awareness pure and simple. If you want to learn more, read Michael Sharp, The Book of Light: The Nature of God, the Structure of Consciousness, and the Universe within You, vol. one -air, 4 vols. (St. Albert, Alberta: Lightning Path Press, 2006).

and the car you drive is that your physical unit has a sophisticated brain and Central Nervous System (CNS) and this brain and CNS is capable, for evolutionary and survival reasons,[68] of operating independently of its own higher self. In other words, your physical unit has a mind of its own.[69] This "mind of its own" feature means that the physical unit can, under certain toxic conditions, operate independently of the wishes of its RMS. That is, the body can do what the spirit does not want it to do! When your physical unit does this, it is exactly as if you were driving in your car and you turned the wheel left but the car, because it had "other ideas," turned right instead.[70] Obviously, if the vehicle does not respond as the driver wishes it to respond, there is a serious problem.

If for whatever reason your physical unit has its own ideas and does not follow the will of its own "higher consciousness," if it makes its own decision in isolation from the Consciousness which animates it, we say it is out of alignment with its RMS. Lack of alignment between your little ego and your big ego, between self and Self, between the car and the intent of the driver, is the root of disjunctive emotions of guilt and shame. *When your physical vehicle is acting out of alignment with its higher Consciousness, higher Consciousness pushes guilt, shame, regret, and other negative emotions to try and communicate the misaligned state.* In serious cases of misalignment and disjuncture, the guilt, shame, and regret can become so painful that the physical unit, specifically the bodily ego, can push higher Consciousness away (specifically "You").

---

[68] Sharp, The Book of the Triumph of Spirit: Master Key.

[69] Neurologically, the "mind" of the body is located in the Default Mode Network (DMN) of the physical brain. Spiritually we may call the mind of the DMN the bodily ego (or little ego) to distinguish it from spiritual ego (a.k.a. big ego). Typically, psychology has focused exclusive attention on the little ego of the physical unit, with no awareness of the larger, and vastly more intelligent, spiritual ego. For more on the DMN see Mike Sosteric, The Science of Ascension: Bodily Ego, Consciousness, Connection, 2016, Available: https://athabascau.academia.edu/DrS.

[70] As a side note, if your car did this, we would say it is broken, get it fixed, or (if it was too costly) buy a new one—something to think carefully about.

When little ego pushes big ego away, when bodily ego shuns **spiritual ego**,[71] you are left in a state of lower consciousness, with a lower **Consciousness Quotient** (CQ).[72] In other words, bodily ego is diminished as a result.

And note, it is not just you that can push. The RMS (i.e. big "Y" you) itself can become uncomfortable with the disjunctive behaviors. Your RMS is a pure reflection of the compassion, power, and glory of Consciousness (i.e. God) and it has difficulty existing in the muck, mire, and mud of a disjunctive world. Thus, if your physical unit is engaged in misaligned and disjunctive behavior, your RMS can be too uncomfortable to make a stronger connection. If the physical unit does not respond to the **signal emotions**[73] of guilt, shame, and regret by changing its actions to be more in alignment with the wishes and intent of its RMS, the RMS may choose not to allow fuller connection, and to gradually withdraw and eventually exit instead. Whether it is the physical unit that is pushing away the RMS, or the RMS that is maintaining a spiritual distance, the result is the same—inability to initiate and/or maintain a connection.

I speak in a lot more detail about alignment and disjuncture later on in the lesson corpus, particularly in LP Book Three and LP Book Four. Here I just want to note that the potential conflict between the actions of your physical unit and the intent and desire of your RMS (your RMS is represented here as the fiery angel in the Halo/Sharp *Passage* card[74]), sets up a bit of a

---

[71] Your spiritual ego is the ego of your higher Self. It is the sense of identity that emerges out of an intensification of consciousness in The Fabric. Spiritual ego may be contrasted with bodily ego, which is the ego that is attached to your physical brain. For more see Sharp, The Book of Light: The Nature of God, the Structure of Consciousness, and the Universe within You. Also http://www.thespiritwiki.com/Spiritual_Ego and http://www.thespiritwiki.com/Bodily_Ego

[72] Consciousness Quotient (CQ) is a number between 0 (dead) and 100 (full) meant to represent the amount of Consciousness present in a physical unit at any given moment. For more see http://www.thespiritwiki.com/CQ

[73] Signal Emotions are emotions your "higher Self" (capital "S" Self) uses to communicate to its physical unit. For more see http://www.thespiritwiki.com/Signal_Emotions

[74] The *Passage* card from the Halo/Sharp deck illustrates an important psychological and emotional dynamic between your RMS and your physical unit. The path illustrates your journey to reconnection and the angel on the

spiritual obstacle. Because the physical unit belongs to the RMS, and because the RMS is the ultimate authority over the physical unit (just like you are the ultimate authority over the car you drive), your physical unit must do what the RMS wants it to do, **otherwise only an attenuated connection will be possible**. The RMS will not abide disjunctive behaviors and it will send clear messages of guilt, shame, and regret in order to push the physical unit to change direction. For your part, you will be unable to cope with powerful guilt and shame. In order to preserve your sanity and avoid the emotional pain, you will push higher consciousness away, effectively turning your back on the "angel" that is your higher self.[75] If you turn your back, you settle back into a state of attenuated disconnection, otherwise known as **normal consciousness**.[76] Or, if you can handle the guilt and shame (perhaps because you have suppressed your emotional responses, as many, in particular men, are taught to do), your own RMS, because it cannot abide the disjunctive acts you engage in, will push itself out and refuse a better connection. Either way you are blocked from entry into the Kingdom of Consciousness.

Unfortunately, this blockage happens all the time, every day, to just about everybody on the planet. The blockage caused by disjuncture, misalignment, and ignorance is powerful, and most people walk around chronically disconnected, experiencing

---

path represents your RMS, in particular the will and intent of your RMS. The Halo/Sharp image represents the idea that in order to progress on the Path your RMS must allow you to pass. Passing is not an issue of struggle, domination, competition, or aggression. Passing is an issue of doing what your RMS wants (i.e. acting in alignment) so that your bodily ego can successfully *merge/connect* with your RMS. In other words, in order to pass you must be in alignment with your RMS. As noted in the main text, I talk more about alignment, disjuncture, and the blocking action of your RMS in the *Book of the Triumph of Spirit* series on planetary archetypes. Also see http://www.thespiritwiki.com/Passage

[75] The dynamic that I am speaking about here is also discussed by Sri Aurobindo in his short work, The Mother. Sri Aurobindo, The Mother (Pondicherry: Sri Aurobido Trust, 2013).

[76] On the LP the phrase normal consciousness refers to the average everyday waking consciousness of your average global citizen. On the LP, average consciousness is not considered particularly healthy or high functioning. In fact, normal consciousness is disconnected consciousness. For more see http://www.thespiritwiki.com/Normal_Consciousness

only brief connections to Consciousness.[77] This is clearly true. If it were not, then we would all be walking around in the permanent bliss of full connection, and clearly we are not. The truth is, misalignment, disjunctive behavior, lack of appropriate training, erroneous ideas and archetypes, and even damage to the mental and emotional apparatus of the physical unit prevent a better connection. If your goal is achieving better connection, that's a lot to do and a lot to overcome, and this is where the Lightning Path comes in. The goal of the Lightning Path is not temporary reconnection, intermittent "mind-blowing" psychedelic experiences, or a one-off mystical experience. *The goal of the LP is complete and permanent reconnection with the glorious Fabric of Consciousness.* Towards that end, the Lightning Path not only provides you with the guidance and direction you need to enable a mystical experience, it also provides you with the direction and support you need to create an environment, and a world, where you can stay permanently connected.

And that, in a nutshell, is the Lightning Path.

---

[77] Abraham Maslow was perhaps the first to note the transient nature of mystical experiences. He said "Some of the effects or after-effects may be permanent but the high moment itself is not." As he himself wisely noted, the transience is not because of the nature of the experience itself, but because "the world" cannot currently support continuous ecstasy and joy. Maslow, "Lessons from the Peak-Experiences," 14.

Doubt, Disbelief, and Disappointment

At this point you may be convinced that the LP has something to offer you, or at least you may be convinced that there is something worth looking at. If so, feel free to skip the rest of this chapter. On the other hand, at this point you might not be convinced. At this point, you might be questioning the integrity of this path or saying to yourself "why bother", "what's the point", or "why the Lightning Path?" If you are asking these questions, that is fine. These are good questions and if you have them, embrace them. There are lots of reasons to doubt, go slow, or even reject what I am saying outright. Perhaps you already have a spirituality and you are perfectly happy with that. Perhaps you have tried this sort of thing before only to be heavily disappointed by what you have found. Perhaps you have put aside religion and spirituality altogether because you feel it is irrational, illogical, superstitious, hypocritical, and even violent. Perhaps you see that despite all the various spiritual systems and traditions that are in place, there aren't too many people walking around in full consciousness and so it must all be a bunch of snake oil and baloney anyhow.

Perhaps, perhaps, perhaps. These are all fair and justified doubts and frankly we (and by "we" I mean the human race) do have a problem. We live in a world where our spiritual "choices" have expanded to the point of embarrassment. Whether it is our local new age book store, our local Christian outlet, or even the free resources of the Internet, we are confronted with a veritable sea of choice. Yet despite all the choice, little seems to change. The world continues on a slide into ecological and economic catastrophe[78] and few people are yet walking around in a state of higher divinity. So, what's up with that? There can only be one answer. Not all paths teach

---

[78] Sharp, The Rocket Scientists' Guide to Money and the Economy: Accumulation and Debt.

you spiritual wisdom, and not all traditional paths (if any at all) lead to reconnection.

This must be true. Despite the cornucopia of spiritual choice, the vast majority of people still live out their lives in normal consciousness. In a world of unfulfilled spiritual promise, who can blame you for wanting to ask some hard questions? So go ahead and ask. And, if you are asking these hard questions, allow me to anticipate some of the questions, objections, and concerns you may have.

To the individual already happy within an established tradition, a light:

If you find yourself reading these words, but you are generally happy in your established spiritual tradition, all I can say is this: no matter what your spiritual tradition is, whether it is Christian or Jewish, Hindu or Buddhist, *The Lightning Path shines a light.* The Lightning Path does this by bringing the teachings into the twenty-first century. Using carefully constructed non-denominational, culturally sensitive, scientifically grounded, and suitably modern conceptualizations, *the Lightning Path clarifies and focuses even the most ancient teachings.* Through the lens of the Lightning Path you will come to understand, with greater depth and precision, **The Word**[79] no matter who uttered it, when it was written, or what tradition you find it in. After learning the concepts and ideas of the Lightning Path, Christians will see the light of God reflected in the words of Christ with renewed clarity. After considering the practices and principles of the LP, Buddhists will see the wisdom and wonder of Gautama. If you are a Gnostic, the LP will clarify and bring into focus the deep truths in your ancient tradition. And this will be true whether you have had a mystical experience or not, and no matter what your home tradition is. Hindu or Freemason, Jew or Protestant, Scientologist or Christian,

---

[79] The phrase "The Word" is used to describe communications that come directly, and without mediation, from your big "S" self, a.k.a. Monadic Consciousness, a.k.a. higher self, also sometimes God. For more, see http://www.thespiritwiki.com/The_Word

normal every-person or experienced high flyer, the end result of your LP study will be renewed interest, renewed faith, renewed certainty, and renewed clarity concerning the valid spiritual truths as they appear in your particular tradition.

Of course, after studying the LP for a while, you may not see everything in your tradition in a positive light. Indeed, after studying the LP you may come to see your own traditions in a new and not altogether flattering light. This is because in addition to exposing the buried truth within your home tradition, *the light of the LP will also expose the confusion, corruption, and distortion that may have been imposed in your tradition over the decades and centuries of its movement in the world.* This is the deeper meaning of the *Lightworker* card from the Halo/Sharp archetype deck, included to the side. The Lightning Path really does shine a light, and the light it shines is the light of pure Consciousness. Underneath this light, that which is hidden is exposed and that which is corrupted or twisted is purified and made straight. This is no idle promise. As you walk the Lightning Path the Light will go off in your brain and you will come to see.

But I have to ask...

...is that a bad thing?

I think not. Even on a good day, shining a light and dispelling the dark is something we should all strive to do. But I have to say, the number of good days is declining. As I discuss in my *Rocket Scientists' Guide to Money and the Economy,* the planet is in increasing psychological, emotional, spiritual, and economic crises. As the crises continues to deepen you want, for your own sake and for the sake of the ones you love, to be able to pluck the pearls of spiritual wisdom from the muck and detritus of confusion, disorientation, and deception no matter how much respect you have for your own spiritual tradition. What's more, you want to be able to do that fast. Things are not improving on this planet, nor will they improve until we all embrace without reservation the Truth and nothing but the

Truth. If you don't shine the light, if you don't clear the darkness, and if you don't embrace the Truth, you and the ones you love will continue to pay the price of this planet's spiraling descent into chaos.

And my point?

Whether you stick with your faith or not does not matter. Do whatever you want. It only matters that you figure out the Truth. In this context, the LP will shine the light and help you sort it all out as fast as you care to do so. You'll see what is good and what is bad; you'll come to distinguish what is right from what is wrong. By studying the LP, you will regain the full light and truth no matter what spiritual tradition in which you currently find yourself residing.

To the individual who has been disappointed in the past, a promise:

If renewed spiritual clarity and discerning and critical spirituality is not enough reason to continue further with the LP, there is another reason and that is simply this; the Lightning Path will not disappoint, and it will not disappoint for several reasons.

Reason one: *the first reason the LP will not disappoint is because it is clear, sophisticated, precise, and <u>open</u>.* Unlike what you may have experienced before, on the LP, there is no esoteric mumbo jumbo, no mystical guesswork, no privileged secrets, no obfuscations, no ridiculous EPMO,[80] and no high costs to prevent you peering directly into the deep inner core. On the LP, no attempts are made to confuse and no bulwarks are built to exclude. On the LP, concepts and ideas are expressed clearly, precisely, and in a way that any adult can understand. What's more, the LP itself is *transparent* like no other spiritual system ever built. On the Lightning Path, you

---

[80] EPMO or Egotistical Polysyllabic Metaphoric Obfuscation is a term I use to describe the intellectual puffery and conceptual cajolery that sometimes passes for spiritual teaching on this planet. See http://www.thespiritwiki.com/EPMO for more details.

won't have to waste time burrowing into the "inner circles", kneeling before altars, or going through hundreds of hours of expensive auditing. On the LP, we find no reason to obscure, dissemble, or otherwise hide. In fact, all LP concepts are defined and openly available on the SpiritWiki,[81] so you can examine the teachings in whatever depth and breadth you choose. On the LP, we throw the doors to the temple wide open and invite everyone inside to have a look at what's going on. *The Lightning Path is the world's first open spiritual system.*

Reason two: *the second reason that the LP will not disappoint is because it won't waste any of your time.* Because the LP is open and because concepts and ideas are clear, grounded, and precise, *you won't have to waste your time trying to sort it all out.* On the LP, you will never have to wonder about the meaning of this concept or that phrase and so you will never have any doubt about the way you wish to proceed. The Lightning Path helps you see the truth clearly and without confusion, misdirection, or hesitation. Instead of wasting time and energy on wondering, worrying, and trying to figure things out, the LP frees your energy for spiritual practice by making your learning process easy. It comes down to simple clarity. If you can see what is on the path and if you can see where it is you are going, you will avoid frustration and doubt, and you will make better progress. On the LP, it won't take lifetimes, decades, or even years, nor will you ever have to stand around wondering if it is working for you. Assuming you approach the materials with an open mind and heart, assuming you are willing to put aside erroneous notions and assumptions that prevent you from making progress (like ethnic, gender, and social class stereotypes), and assuming you stick with it even when it gets a little challenging, you can expect to see rapid enhancements in understanding (i.e. rapid enlightenment) and

---

[81] The SpiritWiki is the canonical glossary of Lightning Path concepts. In that online wiki I provide definitions of all concepts used in the Lightning Path corpus. As noted, some of these concepts are newly minted (like Fabric of Consciousness), and others, like sin, are redefined to consistently reflect the sophistication of LP concepts. Visit the SpiritWiki at http://www.thespiritwiki.com.

rapid improvements in all aspects of your life right from the very start.

And if not, if it turns out to be just a bunch of useless snake oil, you can get out right away and not waste any time! Because the Lightning Path is open, because there are no priests who speak with authority, no masonic masters to whom you must defer, and no popes whose fingers you must kiss, you can peer to the inner core and decide for yourself as quick as a proverbial wink. You will see what the Lightning Path has to offer, see what it is about, and if you don't like what you are seeing, you'll know right away and you can get out without wasting precious breath. If you decide that you don't like what you see, you can exit quickly and painlessly; you'll have no disappointment or regret as result. Wonderful!

Reason Three: *the third reason that the LP will not disappoint is simply because it works. The* goal of authentic spirituality is connection with The Fabric (i.e. authentic mystical connection), and the guidance of the LP puts you in a place and space where healthy and grounded connection experience becomes increasingly likely. Follow the guidance provided, remain open to advice that is offered, put aside prejudice and misunderstandings, and you will achieve powerful and grounded mystical connections, guaranteed. It may not happen tomorrow and you may have a few adjustments to make in your life before you can handle and properly ground your more powerful connection experiences, but if you faithfully follow the guidance, it will happen. The Lightning Path is very effective in this regard. That is, the Lightning Path works.[82] Even though the LP is still "in construction," students report it to be powerful and effective. It helps establish better connections to Consciousness; it helps heal trauma; it helps clear confusion; it puts everything into broad perspective. Indeed, the LP goes a

---

[82] If you want to know what evidence I have, it comes primarily from student feedback directed personally at me, or posted on the LP forums. See http://www.thelightningpath.com/reader-feedback/ for a running log of student feedback. I admit here, more needs to be done by way of scientific validation.

long way towards blasting you forward into a more sophisticated spirituality, and a more grounded and effective mysticism. For this and all the reasons enumerated above, *the LP will not disappoint.*

To the doubting agnostic or atheist, a spark:

The Lightning Path may be interesting to someone already in search for that "something more," and it may tweak the interest of somebody who has searched in the past only to have been disappointed in the end, but does the LP hold anything of value to the atheist who has rejected all consideration of Consciousness, God, Spirit, and "higher" realities? By the same token, does the LP hold any value for the fence sitting agnostic who can't decide one way or another? The answer to this is an unreserved yes. Although the totally closed-minded skeptic will find nothing here but headaches and indigestion, those who still retain their scientific curiosity and those who are still motivated by the search for truth will find a window into an open, rational, and grounded consideration of spiritual and mystical realities that may renew their curiosity about the spiritual side of life. The reason is simple, if a bit egoic. The Lightning Path is created by me, Dr. S. I am both a professional, if slightly unorthodox, scientist and a full-fledged mystic. This unusual and not altogether common blending of perspectives gives the LP a peculiar and powerful potential, if I do say so myself. To put it succinctly, the LP is both logical and spiritual, both empirical and mystical, both rational and divine, both empirical and noetic.[83] The logic and rationality of the LP comes from the fact that I have PhD level training in Sociology. The spiritual, mystical, and divine side comes from the fact that I have over a decade of experience as an active and practicing mystic exploring the hallways of consciousness. *The strength of the LP*

---

[83] Though to be honest, there is nothing irrational about the divine! In fact, if anything, it is more rational and more grounded than anything the little ego (a.k.a. bodily ego) is able to achieve. As Einstein said, the mysterious God expressed in nature revealed "such an intelligence that any human logic falters in comparison" William Hermanns, Einstein and the Poet (Boston: Branden Books, 1983) 83. I will say, higher consciousness is nothing if not pure and unadulterated intelligence.

comes because I have my feet planted firmly in both worlds. As a scientist trained to honor empiricism and logic, I know what it means to research, observe, think, theorize, and report. As a mystic with powerful connection experiences, I know exactly what it means to connect with Consciousness. The mystical experience and scientific training blend nicely. In fact, they strengthen each other. My training as a scientist pushes me to explore, understand, experiment, and evaluate. My training as a mystic encourages me to expand the boundaries of a narrow materialist world view and tap into **noetic**[84] sources of divine wisdom and truth. My training as a scientist makes me uncomfortable with ungrounded belief and "blind faith," yet my experience as a mystic has forced me to be open to phenomena outside the boundaries of visible experience. Putting these two things together is a boundary breaking formula that is productive and self-balancing! My experience as a mystic moderates and balances my narrow scientific materialism and my scientific training moderates and grounds my expansive and celestial mystical experience. In other words, I did not sit down one day, break open my head,[85] spew the resulting mishmash onto paper, and call it divine wisdom, as some mystics might do; neither did I reject and reduce the experiences to mere illusion and delusion, as some scientists might do. Instead, I accepted the validity of mystical experience and worked hard to understand, theorize, and ground the experience. For over a decade I have been diligently writing it all down, sometimes as mystical revelation, and sometimes as scientific analysis, in a challenging attempt to weave an acceptable quilt. The result, I feel, is a rational, logical, fruitful, and satisfying whole.

I have to say, it hasn't been easy. The mystical experiences themselves can often be difficult to understand and

---

[84] Noesis refers to the experience of inner knowledge as special *and* valid knowledge, despite it being purely subjective. The feeling of inner knowledge as special and valid is a common feature of mystical connection experiences. See http://www.thespiritwiki.com/Noesis

[85] Daniel Pinchbeck, Breaking Open the Head: A Psychedelic Journey into the Heart of Contemporary Shamanism (New York: Broadway Books, 2003).

conceptualize in a grounded and modern fashion, and there is the ongoing challenge of blending science and mysticism into an emulsified whole. But the real challenge hasn't been blending the content. Although it is difficult, I find it is possible to blend the two. The real problem is political. The common conception, standard rubric, and powerfully enforced, but unstated, expectation is that science and mysticism go together like water and oil, which is to say, they don't. Typically, you are required either to be a mystic outside of science, or a scientist outside of mysticism. Should you try to be both, you become subjected to ridicule, shaming, and other "boundary maintaining" enforcements. Peter Berger, an illustrious sociologist, draws a strict boundary around religious experience when he writes that religious/mystical experience is "beyond the pale at self-respecting faculty parties", and even insults those who consider the area.[86] I have been shamed for my interests over the years. I even had a colleague call me a space cadet once. And it is not just insults and shaming that scholars like me risk. Rupert Sheldrake, an oxford trained scientist, was ruthlessly excommunicated from the academy for trying to explain naturally observed phenomenon with a non-materialist theory.[87] Knowing that there will be hostility, I have been very reluctant to talk about my mystical side in scientific circles, and very cautious about openly blending the two.

Be that as it may, I have persisted. I continue to write and revise what I have written in an attempt to put it all together, ground it in extant empirical research, and present it in a rational and lucid whole. I've been at it for over a decade and in that time, I have put tens of thousands of hours of thought and effort into the program. The work has involved writing scholarly articles to ground key theoretical planks, creating glossaries of concepts in order to expose the theoretical internals and ensure

---

[86] Peter Berger, <u>The Descularization of the World: Resurgent Religion and World Politics</u> (Grand Rapids MI: Eerdmans, 1999) 4.

[87] A. Freeman, "The Sense of Being Glared At: What Is It Like to Be a Heretic?," <u>Journal of Consciousness Studies</u> 12.6 (2005).

consistency, and writing mystical treatises on the nature of Consciousness and creation. Building from the ground up, I have developed many new concepts and new ideas in order to properly explain and theorize what I, as a mystic, have come to know. In addition, I have had to revise and redefine many old ideas and traditional concepts in order to clarify and purify what to my mind were confused, obscured, and even ideologically tainted spiritual concepts. The whole thing is still very much a work in progress and I have to admit some of the edges are still quite rough, but it is a work that may provide a more reasonable starting point for building a science that is sympathetic to the mystical realities of the universe, and a mystical spirituality that is in tune with the empirical realities identified by modern science. As an atheist or someone hostile to religion and spiritual experience, you may ultimately disagree. Then again, you might not. Maybe if you look, you will find a more balanced, nuanced, rational, and scientifically interesting account of spirituality and mystical realities than you have hitherto thought possible. If you are interested in taking a closer look then all I have left to say is, welcome. I think you will like what you see.

And that is all I have to say on the topic. If I had to boil it down to a few words of logophilic verbal distinction, then to the doubtful, disappointed, disbeliever I'd say, "Chin up." As I, a mystic and scientist, can attest, there is more to the world we live in than the enslaving ideologies of traditional spirituality, and the empty materialism of modern science. If you can put aside your doubt, disappointment, and disbelief just for a little while, you may discover this world for yourself.

Pursuing a Balanced Approach

I would like to note at this juncture, and by way of conclusion, that if you are interested in the scholarly side of this mystical work you must remember, the scholarly side is only one side of the equation, and it is not the most important side. By pursuing the intellectual scholarly side, you may come to understand what I have to say from an intellectual perspective, but this will not give you the profound insight, mystical grounding, or spiritual experience that all experienced mystics will tell you is required if you are to understand and advance. If you really want to understand, you need to experience; therefore, in addition to taking the intellectual route you are also advised to engage in a spiritual practice that seeks authentic connection with The Fabric. In order to do that, you will have to put aside doubt and disbelief, at least for a few moments every day, and get with the program long enough to be able to make the changes that clear the way in order to facilitate the connection. As much as some people might hate to hear this, nevertheless it is true; you can't do it properly without doing the mystical side as well.

I can see where scientists might have problems with this. Modern science decries subjective experience as corrupting, limited, and fraught with potential bias. Scientists are supposed to keep the "I" out of the equation for fear of bias and subjectivity. To an extent, that is true. There are dangers inherent in mixing the blood of scientific inquiry with the milk of mystical experience. Bias and misrepresentation may occur because of self-delusion, self-interest, psychological or emotional pathology, or even political and economic interference. It is a particular problem when it comes to mystical connection, particularly because of the powerful noetic quality of this connection. Because of the noetic nature of connection there is a very real danger that when one connects, one feels special, privileged, and powerful. If one gives in to this pressure, bias, corruption, and a host of other degradations may occur that completely trash the spiritual insight and that may even, in the worst cases, lead to oppression of others, cults, and even mass murder. However, bias, corruption, economic interference, megalomania, and abuse of power is a concern for all areas of human inquiry.[88] Ego and self-interest, if not properly managed, gets in the way in all areas of human endeavor. Even physics suffers from observer bias and it is no great secret that medical researchers struggle mightily to maintain objectivity against the ongoing assaults of the pharmaceutical giants. Indeed, the medical research establishment has a huge problem with corporate influence and bias. It is so bad that some companies are able to influence research enough to get dangerous products on the market![89] Yet this does not stop drug research. Scientists and editors find a way to manage and they trundle forward in objective imperfection. No matter what our area of interest, we all deal with bias. The solution in all cases is not to back down from open inquiry, or to draw arbitrary boundaries around what we can research and how we may become involved, but to jump in with both feet, do the research, and expose the process and findings to the scholarly world. As scholars, we enhance the value of our work and move it toward objective and grounded contribution by showing it off to our colleagues and by inviting their positive suggestions and criticism. When we take an open approach to our scholarly inquiry, the issue of bias and self-delusion takes care of itself.

Now, the point here is not to go into any great depth about the value and dangers of participant or ethnographic research, or bias in science, mysticism, and religion; the point is to simply highlight the fact that being directly involved in the mystical process does not invalidate the process. You can be a participant and still understand the process from an academic perspective. In fact, it is possible to argue that being a participant opens you up to a greater depth and breadth of perspective than would be possible to the outside observer.[90] In

---

[88] For example, I know professors who have abused their status to have sex with students much younger.

[89] Peter Whoriskey, "As Drug Industry's Influence over Research Grows, So Does the Potential for Bias," The Washington Post 2012.

[90] In fact, this is exactly what I would argue. I funded my way through graduate school by working as a bartender in

any case, the point here is that you don't have to remain independent to affect objectivity. In fact, it is ridiculous to suggest that you have to, or that you even can. We all struggle with personal and professional attachments and our world is inevitably and forever subjective. Objectivity, getting outside our own solipsistic spaces, is always a work in progress and we should not shy away from the work just because it is work, or because it is always in progress.

In closing, I have this to say. Whether you are a scientist or scholar interested in the phenomenon of mystical experience or simply an interested spiritual seeker, take a balanced approach by keeping your feet in both worlds. Pursue authentic mystical experience, but keep it grounded, sane, and rational. Get you connected to You, but stay linked closely to empirical realities. Ultimately, these two worlds are not incompatible. Ultimately, these two worlds are exactly the same. It is only our view of things, our training, and the dogmatic ideology spewing from those who would keep us separated and disconnected[91] that separates the two and makes them seem different. Moving forward from here, we must blend the two worlds. The LP provides a perspective and an avenue for doing just that. This is important! Despite all the evils perpetrated in the name of religion, despite the ongoing attempts to contain mystical experience, reduce it to irrelevance, or turn it into an instrument that serves the status quo, it is in this blending that the hope of our future lies.

---

a nightclub. When I entered a PhD program I used my experience in the nightclub where I worked to write a paper on the nightclub labour process entitled *Subjectivity and the Labour Process.* The article was, for a time, a hotly debated contribution to labour process theory. It is a contribution whose depth and breadth was made possible only because I was a participant in the cultural milieu of the club. An "objective" scientific observer would never have been able to generate the insights I was able to generate. See Mike Sosteric, "Subjectivity and the Labour Process: A Case Study in the Food and Beverage Industry," Work, Employment, and Society 10.2 (1996).

[91] I speak more about this dominant ideology in my *Book of the Triumph of Spirit* series. In that series, I explore the dominant, elite ideology and how it has been constructed to keep us oppressed and disconnected from our true spiritual glory.

Reconnecting with The Fabric

If you are still reading at this point you know what the LP is about, you know about reconnection with The Fabric, and you know that the LP strives for a balanced, modern, and *practical* approach to mystical connection. The purpose of the Lightning Path isn't to yap at you about your divine self, to merely describe the high spiritual realities, to proselytize and preach to you about it, or to point in a gawking and worshipful (or disdainful) manner toward those who have had the realizations. The purpose is to lead <u>you</u> to experience and know for yourself the high truth of your glorious spiritual divinity. Put another way, the Lightning Path is a spiritual system designed to guide you toward authentic, safe, and powerful spiritual/mystical experiences. I know I am being repetitive when I say this, but I'll repeat it anyway. Following the LP leads you toward a mystical connection with the powerful realities of Consciousness that form the foundation of our realities, and this creation.

In this lesson, I want to go a bit deeper into the practical aspect of the LP, specifically the goal of connection itself and how the LP accomplishes its goal. As far as the goal of reconnection goes, it might seem odd to some people to suggest that reconnecting with The Fabric is the goal of authentic spirituality and the LP. Many of us have been told for example that spirituality is about "following the rules" (i.e. commandments), going to church, and kneeling in a pew. Many of us have also been told that the successful outcome of spirituality is to be found in post-mortem entry into heaven, or in karmic graduation to a higher life in the next karmic round. In modern consumerist society, some people have even debased spirituality to consumer idolatry (as if putting an angel you bought at Walmart on your Christmas tree really makes you more spiritual) and the venal pursuit of "abundance" (read money and profit). But these are not the goals of authentic spirituality. These goals are nothing more than intentionally seeded distractions from the true goal which is simply realization of your divine self. These distractions serve the interests of those who turn you away from true religious/mystical experience, but they have nothing at all to do with an authentic mystical connection. The point of practicing any spiritual technique, whether that is prayer, transcendental meditation, Sufi spinning, or entheogen induced connection, is direct comprehension and experience of divine realities. This is the point of our collective drive for spiritual truth and it is the goal of authentic spiritual/religious practice. Everything else, from karmic rehabilitation through entry via the "pearly gates," is absolutely and one hundred percent irrelevant.

If I have convinced you to put aside the distractions that are thrown at you for a moment, and if I have tweaked your interest about reconnection with **The Fabric**,[92] that still doesn't leave us on a solid spiritual footing. I am not the only one, after all, to say that reconnection with some sort of "higher reality" is the goal. Others have said it as well. Indeed, if you go beneath the distracting surface of organized religion and move beyond its goals of subservience, karmic rehabilitation, and so on, you often find "gurus," master masons, Golden Dawn magicians, and others who make it their mission to speak about higher realities. The problem with these people is that they often speak of mystical connection as a major cosmic challenge that requires decades of yogic, meditative, or intentional effort. For folks[93] like this, achieving connection is a major life attainment that isn't even guaranteed in the end. You can struggle and fight your entire life but never attain the Holy Grail, which is the filling of the cup with the water of Consciousness. For these people the path is hard, torturous, prone to disappointment, and open to repeated failure.

---

[92] The Fabric is short for The Fabric of Consciousness (FOC). The FOC is a term coined by yours truly in *The Book of Light* to represent the collective reality of divine consciousness. There is no point in trying to explain it here. For a full run down see my four volume *Book of Light* series http://www.thespiritwiki.com/Book_of_Light

[93] The word I really want to use here is "fools."

But is that true? Is the path to reconnection really as difficult as some people say? The answer to that question, in my opinion, is no. When you get right down to it, reconnecting with The Fabric is not all that difficult. Oh sure, people preach that mystical experience is difficult, and to be sure there are challenges, but it is not as hard as some might have you believe.[94] In fact, I would argue that all of us are capable of mystical connection. Indeed, under healthy familial, social, and global conditions, mystical connection can be easily facilitated. We might even say, in fact we shall say, that under healthy conditions mystical experience occurs naturally, even inevitably! The only real issues behind successful mystical practice are the exact same issues behind healthy, happy, life experiences. *If you want to experience union with Consciousness, protect your fragile physical unit from damage, heal the damage that has already been done to it, strive to achieve alignment, and practice techniques of union.* If you protect, heal, align, and practice techniques of union, Consciousness descends easily and naturally. Of course, dealing with Consciousness as it descends is another matter. Indeed, dealing with consciousness descending can be quite the challenge; however, as far as making a connection goes, getting a glimpse, and realizing some truth, it is not that hard. This is the whole point of the Lightning Path, at the basic level at least. The whole point of the LP is to help you protect your physical unit, help you heal previous damage, and help you achieve mystical alignment with your bright, brilliant Consciousness so

---

[94]"Why would people want to work to deny mystical experience to others? For two reasons. Reason one, they want to block your progress so they can preserve the current *regime of accumulation.* The foundation for this claim is set out in the *Rocket Scientists* Guide to Money and the Economy. Reason two, they want to block it because of the revolutionary outcome of authentic spirituality! As I argue in my article *Slavery, Mysticism, and Transformation,* transformative mystical experience often leads to dramatic political, moral, and spiritual shifts. To be as blunt as possible, these shifts can be a problem for the status quo. Thus the status quo recognizes this potential and works hard to prevent it. If they cannot prevent it, they channel and control the outcome of mystical connection. Mike Sosteric, Dangerous Memories: Slavery, Mysticism, and Transformation, Unpublished Manuscript, 2016, Academia.edu, Available: https://www.academia.edu/25031557/Dangerous_memories_-_Slavery_mysticism_and_transformation, 7/20 2016, Sosteric, Dangerous Memories: Slavery, Mysticism, and Transformation.

that it can easily and smoothly descend into the vessel.

Now, you may doubt that mystical experience is such an easy thing to facilitate, but you don't have to take my word for it. William Harmless,[95] who teaches a course on mysticism, relates a profound moment for him when one of the students in his class, after spending several weeks studying mystics and mysticism, raised her hand and said:

> I don't want to sound arrogant or anything, but you know- when I read these people, I think that I've experienced something like that. I am beginning to think that I'm a mystic—maybe, not the same way these people are, maybe not as intensely. But I know what they're talking about.

Harmless goes on...

> There was a pause, then hand after hand began to rise. Each who spoke repeated something similar. These mystics were talking about things that they themselves had tasted, that they too had felt.[96]

Harmless never gives us any indication how many students in his class reported mystical experience, but it is interesting that before this one girl spoke up, people were silent about their experiences. It took weeks of open discussion, plus the brave admission of one female, to get people to admit they had mystical connections!

A reasonable question to ask at this point is just how many people have mystical connection experiences but are too afraid to admit it or talk about it? As surprising as it might at first sound to some, scientists have an idea. Conservative estimates put the number anywhere between thirty and fifty percent,[97] but

---

[95]William Harmless, Mystics (New York: Oxford University Press, 2008).

[96]Harmless, Mystics ix-x.

[97]David Yamane and Megan Polzer, "Ways of Seeing Ecstasy in Modern Society: Experiential-Expressive and Cultural-Linguistic Views," Sociology of Religion 55.1 (1994).

some scholars, myself included, feel that just about everyone has had a mystical connection experience at one time or another. Abraham Maslow, one of the most famous American Psychologists of all time, was perhaps the first one to point out just how common mystical experiences really are. Speaking of the difference between people who have mystical experience (people he called "**peakers**" after his concept of the peak experience) and people who do not ("**non-peakers**" as he called them), Maslow said:

> In my first investigations ... I thought some people had peak-experiences and others did not. But, as I gathered information and as I became more skillful in asking questions, I found that a higher and higher percentage of my subjects began to report peak-experiences.... I finally fell into the habit of expecting everyone to have peak-experiences and of being rather surprised if I ran across somebody who could report none at all. Because of this experience, I finally began to use the word "non-peaker" to describe, not the person who is unable to have peak-experiences, but rather the person who is afraid of them, who suppresses them, who denies them, who turns away from them, or who "forgets" them.[98]

As you can see, given how natural the process seems to be, and how common mystical experiences are, the topic of mystical connection with The Fabric of Consciousness is not so strange after all. What is perhaps more strange is that, given how common mystical experiences are, we don't talk about them more often than we do. When you think about it, our global silence on the topic is puzzling, even bizarre! If everybody has had one (or more), yet nobody talks about them, then from where does our collective silence on the topic arise?

A conservative estimate is 50%! This is certainly something to think about. In fact, next time you find yourself in a group of random people, ask yourself, how many of these people have had a mystical experience. A very conservative answer is at least 50%. When you have fully apprehended the significance of that fact, ask yourself, if it is that common, why does no one talk about it?

[98]Maslow, "The "Core-Religious" or "Transcendent" Experience," 340-1.

The answer to that question is easy. We don't talk about it because we have been actively silenced. We have been silenced by secular atheists who take it as a given that we live in a material universe and who ascend the pulpit to arrogantly pontificate their truth and scornfully ridicule those whom they oppose (i.e. those that believe there is something more). We are silenced out of fear of ridicule. Richard Dawkins is perhaps the most famous of the arrogant atheist pontificators, but they exist all around. A colleague in my university once called me a "space cadet," and quite recently I was approached by an internet troll working for an online podcast entitled *The Atheist Experience.* These trolls were out actively trolling Twitter and other social media looking for people willing to phone into their show and be lambasted as the faithful fools that they were. I kid you not; these people were actively looking for victims to persecute.

Of course, it is not only fear of persecution that stops us from talking about it. Abraham Maslow suggested that we don't talk about mystical experience because we suppress it, repress it, misrepresent it, or reject it as such because of milder bias and prejudice taught to us, I would say, by overly rational authorities and pessimistic pundits. We experience toxic socialization and are trained to be, and as a result become, pessimistic, overly rational, and even obsessional. We are taught to see mystical experience as weakness, irrationality, even as madness. As a consequence, we reject for no other reason than personal bias and prejudice. I'll leave it to Maslow to underline the point.

> At first it was our thought that some people simply didn't have peaks. But, as I said above, we found out later that it's much more probable that the non-peakers have them but repress or misinterpret them, or-for whatever reason-reject them and therefore don't use them. Some of the reasons for such rejection so far found are: (1) a strict Marxian attitude, as with Simone de Beauvoir, who was persuaded that this was a weakness, a sickness (also Arthur Koestler). A Marxist should be "tough." Why Freud rejected his is anybody's guess: perhaps (2) his

19th century mechanistic-scientific attitude, perhaps (3) his pessimistic character. Among my various subjects I have found both causes at work sometimes. In others I have found (4) a narrowly rationalistic attitude which I considered a defense against being flooded by emotion, by irrationality, by loss of control, by illogical tenderness, by dangerous femininity, or by the fear of insanity. One sees such attitudes more often in engineers, in mathematicians, in analytic philosophers, in bookkeepers and accountants, and generally in obsessional people.[99]

All these things combine in the following example. Many years ago, a friend of mine came forward with an experience he had. He was watching the movie *Master and Commander* and suddenly he had powerful, visceral, and undeniable memories from a past life spent swashbuckling on the high seas. His approach to me was sheepish and cautious and while I strongly confirmed the reality of past lives for him, nevertheless he requested that we keep the discussion between he and I private. As a university graduate, avowed atheist, and rationalist rejecter of all delusional spirituality, he didn't want any of his friends to know he was seriously considering a spiritual topic. I'm sure he felt that he would have looked stupid and that his friends would have made fun of him. He anticipated negativity and persecution, felt it might be delusion and/or madness, and as a result, he silenced himself and never spoke of it again! And I know he is not alone. Many have had mystical type connection experiences but are just too afraid to talk about them. How many other people out there have mystical/religious experiences but either refuse to talk about or even work to erase their experience(s) from consciousness is hard to say. This is obviously a research question; but, if we look, we are very likely to find that many people either do not recognize their experiences as mystical, don't bother to talk about them out of

---

[99] Maslow, "Lessons from the Peak-Experiences."

fear, or actively deny that they ever had them at all. When it comes to authentic mystical experiences, people have been silenced.

At this point I'd like to return us back to a consideration of the Lightning Path. The Lightning Path is certainly about achieving mystical connection or union. The argument in this section has been that once you get past the distractions, and despite propaganda to the contrary, mystical union isn't as difficult as some people make it out to be. There is evidence that this is true in the ubiquity of the experience itself. We don't know this because we have been silenced. But if we weren't silenced, and if all those who had mystical experience felt free to talk about them, we would know, from our own experience and the experiences of those around us, that mystical experience, what I would call connection experience or connection to The Fabric, is more common, and more straightforward, than we have been led to believe. It would be undeniable, really.

So where does that leave us?

Accepting for the moment that mystical connection is something that we want to do, and bringing ourselves back to the claim that the Lightning Path is a pathway, a set of ideas and techniques, designed to facilitate mystical connection, the next question is, "How does the LP facilitate reconnection?" On this topic, there is a lot to say and to be frank, the answer to the question is developed in the broad expanse of the LP corpus. So, to even suggest that I can provide a complete answer to that question in anything like a digestible little information byte is delusion. In this book, which is intended as an introduction to the LP, I will only speak in general terms. Speaking generally however, *there are six things that the LP does to encourage mystical experience*. The LP:

1. clears a path,

2. modernizes the teachings,

3. purifies the truth,

4. highlights the importance of psychological, emotional, and physical health,

5. builds a solid practical foundation for advancement and experience, and

6. builds a support network.

Let us spend a few moments discussing each of these contributions, starting with the cleared pathway.

Clearing a Path

The first thing that the Lightning Path does to encourage mystical experience and connection with The Fabric is to clear a path. That is, the *Lightning Path clears the way of the obstacles and blockages that prevent your awakening and activation.* I can tell you now, but you will understand more fully later, that this is a big deal. Many things have been put in your way to prevent your spiritual awakening and empowerment and *the most significant thing you can do to guarantee spiritual progress is to clear those blockages away.* The truth is that many misconceptions, misdirections, misperceptions, and even deceptions have been placed in your path with the express intent of preventing your spiritual awakening. The misconception, misdirection, and deception makes it extremely difficult for all except the most dedicated and isolated aspirant to make meaningful forward progress. With all the chunks on the road it can literally take decades to sort it all out. That's OK though. The Lightning Path has been designed to circumvent obstacles, overcome deception, and make it easier to understand and move forward. It does this by:

a) stripping away superfluous details that distract and confuse,

b) clearing away misconceptions and deceptions that have accumulated over the centuries and that block you from spiritual understanding and advancement, and

> c) providing you with clear, logical, precise, and grounded guidance.

Put all these together and you have a system of spiritual awakening that does exactly what it says it does; it shines a light that guides your way home.

Of course, the Lightning Path isn't a miracle system. Rapid transformation can occur, but even so, you can't simply wave a magical mystical wand, sit on a crystal, or rub a singing bowl and be magically transported to the kingdom of high Consciousness (otherwise known as the **Kingdom of Heaven**).[100] *The LP cannot magically overcome a toxic or misaligned environment,* for example, and you have to do the work. As we will explore in more detail as we progress, if your work or personal life is filled with anger, hatred, toxicity, negativity, various forms of violence (emotional, psychological, physical, or spiritual), and other forms of misaligned behaviors, you'll have a hard time making a connection and an even harder time making it persistent. Beyond that, there is the actual work involved. There is no way around it, you have to study. You have to read the books, learn the concepts, understand the teachings, and practice the preaching. You have to be a fully aware and motivated participant in your own awakening, activation, and ascension. If you are not aware, motivated, and active, if you don't do what you need to do to move yourself forward, if you don't clean up your toxic environments, and if you just sit on a crystal or rub a singing bowl once in a while, then even the most magical representation of spiritual truth will not help you. *No matter how pure and pristine the path before you, if you want to move forward, you are going to have to walk, run, or crawl.* If you just sit there looking down the path, or sit down and play with singing bowls, nothing mystical is going to happen.

---

[100] The Kingdom of Heaven (a.k.a. the Kingdom of God) is the Christian term for a state of the physical unit characterized by strong and persistent Connection. The Kingdom of God represents a state of "high" Consciousness in body. See http://www.thespiritwiki.com/Kingdom_of_Heaven

Modernizing the Teachings

The second way the Lightning Path contributes to your spiritual awakening and activation is that it brings spiritual teachings into the twenty-first century. Rather than relying on the ideas and teachings of medieval mystics or ancient Buddha's, the Lightning Path provides concepts, ideas, and techniques tailored to the modern mind and suitable for modern sensibilities. This is, once again, significant and important. Using ancient wisdom to fuel modern spiritual awakening is always problematic. Different mental sets, different circumstances, different cultural contexts, and even antique superstitions make communications from the ancients (or even communications from people a hundred years ago) difficult, sometimes even impossible to properly understand. In the best of cases, ancient communications can take time to sort out. You can read about a spiritual concept or idea, but struggle to wrap your head around it. But, that's in the best of cases. Many problems conspire to make understanding ancient spiritual guidance, even guidance provided by a certified spiritual master like Pantanjali, problematic. For example, ancient texts always have to be translated, and translations are problematic at the best of times. Not only does the translator need to be absolutely familiar with both languages (and who, we may ask, is absolutely familiar with an ancient version of Greek, Sanskrit, or Aramaic), but the translator also needs to be knowledgeable and sophisticated about the topic at hand, otherwise they won't be able to fully understand, and they may introduce error or personal bias.[101] Far better in this context is to rely on modern materials written with modern sensibilities and aimed at a modern mind set.

Besides the problems associated with dated and translated materials, there are also *massive cultural differences that might*

---

[101] This is more common than you might think. I haven't found what I consider to be a good or accurate translation of Pantanjali's Union (Yoga) Sutras. They all seem to be off in one way or another.

impede understanding. The best example of a cultural difference that impedes understanding is an idiom. An idiom is simply a combination of words whose meaning is separate from the literal meaning of the words. Idioms seem to say one thing (or seem to say nothing logical at all), but really say something else altogether. All cultures have idioms. For example, if I said that I quit smoking "cold turkey," anybody from my culture would understand exactly what I mean by that, but people from other cultures may not be so clear about it. They may figure it out if they think about it long enough or research it online, but there is no guarantee that they will understand the concept straight out of the gate. Yet this is exactly what we expect when we read the teachings of ancient masters and **Avatars**.[102] When we read these old teachings, we expect to be able to understand them properly at their word (sometimes at their literal word), but we often don't. For example, the phrase "Kingdom of Heaven" is obviously an idiom. It represents a concept or idea that is not directly related to the literal meaning of the words. If you were an ancient citizen of Nazareth, a traveler with Christ, or a child that grew up in the culture, you may have easily understood what Christ meant by the phrase; unfortunately, the same cannot be said of a modern Christian. A modern Christian cannot know for sure what Christ meant. Unless they have experienced a profound connection event for themselves, that is, unless they have experienced the "Kingdom of Heaven" for themselves, they will always be dependent on somebody else's word, or best guess. You can go to a Church and listen to a priest explain it, but has the priest experienced high consciousness and does he or she really understand? Or, is she or he just blowing it out their arse? Similarly, you can pick up a book in a new age book store to try and figure it out, but has the author really made a connection and even if they have, are

---

[102] On the LP we define an avatar as follows: An avatar is any master teacher (usually, but not always a spiritual teacher) who has a strong and pure connection to Consciousness, whose life is devoted exclusively to dissemination of The Message, and who encourages and supports individual and collective Realization. For more, see http://www.thespiritwiki.com/Avatar

they truly wise in the ways of Spirit? Given the linguistic and cultural distance between you and Jesus Christ, you have to ask the critical questions, otherwise you risk being dragged off the path and down some dead end byway. In this context, it is reasonable to suggest that modern mystical wisdom penned by a modern mystical way shower who is familiar with modern cultural idioms and modern mental sensibilities is a far better way to approach your study. The short of it is, using a modern system like the Lightning Path can save you time, effort, and frustration (not to mention money).

Just saying.

Purifying the Truth

As you can see, there are problems, but chunks on the path, poor translations, and dated spiritual concepts are not the only issues. Deception, intentional misdirection, and active efforts to contain the transformative potentials of mystical experience also figure into the mix.[103] The truth is that there are many people on this Earth who do not want you to know the truths of Consciousness and creation. There are many people who would keep you in the dark about your true light and glory. For example, all the great spiritual masters and Avatars say exactly the same thing about who you are. They say that you are a God and they say it quite directly. Jesus said it in a number of places.

> **John 10:34**. Is it not written in your law, "I have said you are gods."

> **Corinthians 3:16** Know ye not that ye are the temple of God, and that the Spirit of God dwelleth in you?

Mohammed said it when he said that "He who knows his self knows God." St Catherine of Genoa said it when she said "My

---

[103]Grace M Jantzen, Power, Gender, and Christian Mysticism (New York: Cambridge University Press, 1995). Also Sosteric, Dangerous Memories: Slavery, Mysticism, and Transformation.

Me is God, nor do I recognize any other Me[104] except my God himself." Even Meister Eckhart, a very famous medieval mystic, and one who briefly flirted with the appellation of heretic,[105] said it over and over and over again.[106] The problem is, some people don't want you to know this basic truth because if you really knew and understood who you were, you wouldn't, as St. John of the Cross says, be satisfied with the "crumbs from the Father's table."[107] *If you knew the Truth, you would expect more, not only for yourself, but for all the people of this world.* The truth is, if you truly understood who you really are, you would look at the world around you and you would demand, work for, and eventually accomplish total global transformation. You would, as St. John of the Cross says, exalt in your own glory and transform the world around you.

> Mine are the heavens and mine is the earth. Mine are the nations, the just are mine and mine the sinners. The angels are mine, and the Mother of God, and all things are mine; and God himself is mine and for me, because Christ is mine and all for me. What do you ask, then, and seek, my soul? Yours is all of this, and all is for you. Do not engage yourself in something less, nor pay heed to the crumbs which fall from your Father's table. Go forth and exult in your Glory! Hide yourself in It and rejoice, and you will obtain the deepest desires of your heart.

This total global transformation would be a good thing for the masses and the planet, but a bad thing for the privileged few

---

[104] Me with a capital "M" is used to distinguish your real Self, your true Self, your divine Self, from your bodily self.

[105] Harmless, Mystics.

[106] I keep a list of the "you are God" sayings of the mystics, masters, and Avatars at http://www.michaelsharp.org/about-you/. Check it out.

[107] This revolutionary nature of authentic mystical experience is discussed in Sosteric, Dangerous Memories: Slavery, Mysticism, and Transformation.

who benefit from your ignorance of **Self**.[108] So, instead of telling you the Truth, the people who want you to be "satisfied with the crumbs" lie, dissemble, and twist the teachings to turn you away from authentic mystical experience. Couple this deception with translation errors, cultural idioms, and other problems and it can be quite a challenge to sort it all out. Not to worry though because not only does the Lightning Path update and modernize the teachings, it presents them in a way that doesn't compromise the Truth for profit or political interest. *The goal of the Lightning Path is nothing more nor less than your full and unrestricted connection to The Fabric of Consciousness and your full realization of the truth of your divine glory.* Thus, on the Lightning Path, you can be sure that the direction you are going in is the direction that has been intended by all spiritual masters of the past. On the Lightning Path, you can be sure that you are moving toward a realization of your powerful glory and divinity. There are no compromises on this path and no political, economic, or ideological strings attached. This is all a great benefit because not only does it speed you on your way, it also means you do not have to wonder and worry. Instead of fretting about the meaning of ancient concepts, errors in translation, cultural idioms, or the peculiar corruptions imposed by those dominated by their own venal political or economic self-interest, all you have to do is focus on the teachings and choose. Stay at your "normal" level of consciousness and do "normal" level things with your life if that is what you want, or advance toward the powerful and glorious divinity that is you. The meaning is there; the message and teachings are pure and clear; the choice is yours. How easy is that?

---

[108] The word "Self" with a capital "S" refers to your Spiritual Ego. The word "self" with a small "s" refers to your Bodily Ego. Self is also known as Atman, Christ self, etc. To explore in more detail, see http://www.thespiritwiki.com/Self

Encouraging Strength and Health

So far, we have seen how the Lightning Path helps you along your way by clearing a path, modernizing the teachings, and staying close to the mystical truth. The fourth way that the Lightning Path contributes to your spiritual awakening and activation is that it highlights the damaging effect of physical, emotional, psychological, and even spiritual violence, and it *focuses and points you in the general direction of emotional, psychological, and physical healing.* This might not sound like a big deal at first, but it is. The truth is, most religions and spiritualties have nothing to say about the physical and mental health of your body and mind. In fact, most spiritual systems (whether they be traditional Catholic, ancient Buddhist, or modern New Age, New Thought varieties), find excuses to justify shit and abuse. As perverse as it really is, we the people of this Earth are led to believe that violence and abuse are in fact good for us. We all experience violence, abuse, and neglect as the result of a toxic socialization process that we endure, but we all pretend it doesn't matter (or worse, that it actually benefits us), and we all make excuses for that abuse. *On this Earth, we have a perverse ideology that encourages us to accept damaging violence.* The ideology finds perfect expression in the spiritual meme "what doesn't kill us makes us stronger," or in the "spiritual wisdom" (read spiritual ideology) you can find printed on Starbuck's coffee cups "No Experience is ever wasted: everything has meaning." We are taught, essentially, that no experience, not even a violent experience, is a bad experience. Everything, from economic exploitation to rape and abuse has utility for your "growth plan." In a single puff of ideological smoke decades, nay centuries, of physical, emotional, psychological, and spiritual abuse become God's (or Nature's) special plan for us!

There is no other word for it except to say that this is absurd. We would never argue that a broken bone, a smashed skull, or a concussion addled brain "builds character," but when it comes to emotional, psychological, and spiritual abuse, we think repeated violent skull smashing makes us better people! We think this because **Agents of Consciousness**[109] feed us these ideological memes which get us to view our abuse as salutatory and positive, and they are effective. By the time we are adults, we look back on our abusive, sometimes horrific, childhood experiences with actual fondness and pride! "My experiences," we say to ourselves, "made me what I am today." Within the rubric of this twisted ideology, we sugar coat our suffering and normalize profound emotional, psychological, and spiritual damage; damage, it should be noted, that makes connection more difficult! It doesn't matter how horrific the abuse might be, thanks to the ideology decanted into our mind, we find a way to elevate it to a divine gift. Even Hollywood gets in on the nonsense. A movie entitled *Whiplash* is a horrifying glorification of the toxic abuse experienced by one drummer at the hands of an emotionally and psychologically violent orchestra director. The general message of the movie was that horrifying abuse was in fact necessary to train the professional drummer! The message was clear. Abuse provides motivation and direction! Abuse helps us to grow! Over and over again we hear the ideological mantra— "what doesn't kill you makes you stronger." We accept the doublespeak that *abuse = growth* and then, through the twisted glass of ideology, we reinterpret our negative experience as if it is positive and salutatory.

Our reinvention of abuse as salutatory instruction can get quite bizarre. I remember once having a conversation with a self-styled guru who said that we choose all our experiences and that all our experiences help us grow. When I asked him if this included the abuse of children, he said yes. When I pointed

---

[109] An **agent** of consciousness is an agent of socialization whose specific purpose is to insert ideas and archetypes into the individual and collective consciousness of this planet. Writers, directors, advertising agents, school teachers, parents, news reporters, university professors, and any other individual involved in the transmission of archetypes through song, dance, news, education, etc., may be considered an Agent of Consciousness. See http://www.thespiritwiki.com/Agents_of_Consciousness

out the statistics on pedophilia and child rape and asked if children chose to be raped and sometimes murdered by abusive men and women, he said yes!?! When I asked him what possible benefit could come from such an experience, he said he didn't know because, of course, "who can know the mind of God."[110] Nevertheless, he was certain that there was some learning experience buried in there somewhere.

As I said above, the Lightning Path does not buy into this spiritual ideology at all. Rather than defending violence and abuse, which as we progress in our studies we will see actually disconnects us from Consciousness, the Lightning Path takes issue with it. The Lightning Path's position is that we, and by "we" I mean all humans on this planet, have incurred, as a result of a very toxic socialization process, a lot of damage to our physical unit. We often experience physical violence ("spare the rod and spoil the child," as the Bible says) and we almost always encounter repeated instances of emotional, psychological, and even spiritual abuse. *The Lightning Path encourages you to see that the violence is far more pervasive than you might initially think, and far more damaging than you have been led to believe.* As I note in a short research article on the topic of toxic socialization, the impact of forms of violence and abuse on the mental, emotional, spiritual, and even physical well-being of the victim is profound.[111] The damage can be severe and obvious as is the case when we deal with personality disorders, eating disorders, or emotional disorders; or, the damage can be subtle and hard to detect, as for example when we deal with the bodily rejection of higher consciousness, as discussed earlier. Severe and obvious or subtle and hard to detect doesn't matter. The truth is, violence, especially emotional, psychological, and spiritual violence, hurts us, damages us, and makes reconnection with the Fabric

---

[110] Of course, the answer to the question "who can know the mind of God?" is *you*. We can all know the mind of God if we pursue authentic mystical connection.

[111] For a summary of the profoundly debilitating impact of toxic socialization, see Michael Sharp, Toxic Socialization, 2016, The SpiritWiki, Available: http://www.thespiritwiki.com/Toxic_Socialization, January 15 2016.

of Consciousness, re-entry into the Kingdom of Heaven, or whatever you want to call it, difficult. I know I'm being repetitive here, but it is important you get this into your head. If your intent is reconnection with the Fabric of Consciousness, then you have to know that *violence and abuse undermines the integrity of your mind and body and creates emotional and psychological wounds and scars that make the re-connection (i.e. the descent of consciousness into vessel) problematic.*

And should this really be a surprise? If you take a modern sports car and hit it with hammers, beat it with clubs, and drive it hard through the downtown streets of your city, it will deteriorate. Your physical unit is far more advanced and sensitive than a hunk of metal and if you allow it to be hurt and damaged, either through physical abuse, name calling, ridicule, shaming, etc., you will have difficulties being happy and productive, and you will experience problems when you try to connect with higher consciousness. Your *body and mind, your physical unit, is a fine tuned instrument for the high power consciousness of God.* If that body and mind is not maintained properly or worse, if it is damaged, you will experience challenge and difficulty in the area of mystical connection.

It is in the context of the damage that we experience as a result of toxic socialization that the LP focus on strength and healing comes into play. On the Lightning Path, you will find no ideological excuses for violence and abuse. On the LP, you will find no slick and sophisticated propaganda designed to get you to accept hurt and pain as beneficial. On the Lightning Path, you are encouraged not only to see the violence and abuse for what it is (i.e. damaging to the mind and body), but also to take steps to stop the abuse and heal any damage that has been done so you can strengthen to a point where you can handle the high power consciousness of The Fabric.[112]

---

[112] Michael Sharp, Lightning Path Workbook Four - Foundations, Lightning Path Workbook Series, ed. Michael Sharp, vol. 4 (St. Albert, Alberta: Lightning Path Press, Unpublished), Michael Sharp, Lightning Path Book Two -

It is important.

If we don't recognize that damage has been done, if we don't understand that this damage can make reconnection difficult, and if we don't take steps to stop the abuse and heal the damage, our efforts to reconnect will be ineffectual and ultimately unsuccessful. Don't forget this.

Building a Foundation

So far we have discussed removing obstacles, modernizing the teachings, purifying the truth, and healing as things the LP does to facilitate authentic connection. The fifth way that the Lightning Path contributes to your spiritual awakening is that it provides a proper and safe foundation for grounded and sensible connection, and the spiritual awakening that inevitably ensues. This foundation is important. Those who have researched the topic of mystical and religious experience will know that mysticism has a long association with psychosis and madness. Indeed, the notion that mysticism and madness are related goes all the way back to Socrates who suggested that "madness" was a divine gift.[113] More recently, Sigmund Freud believed that the "oceanic feeling" that mystics often report was simply a regression, and others have agreed. William James, a psychologist quite supportive of mystical experience, said that:

> Religious mysticism is only one half of mysticism. The other half has no accumulated traditions except which the textbooks on insanity supply. Open any one of these and you will find abundant cases in which "mystical ideas" are cited as characteristic symptoms of enfeebled or deluded states of mind.[114]

Foundations Lightning Path Lesson Series, ed. Michael Sharp, vol. 2 (St. Albert, Alberta: Lightning Path Press, 2013).

[113] E. R. Dodds, The Greeks and the Irrational (Berkeley: University of California Press, 1951).

[114] James, The Varieties of Religious Experience: A Study of Human Nature 426.

In this century, a clear link has been established between mental illness and mystical experience as such.[115] This is not to say that mystical experiences are madness, but just that there are linkages. Scholars themselves don't have a very good understanding of what those linkages are I'm afraid, but I can tell you that mystical experience can descend into madness and that this mystical madness is a problem more likely to manifest when

a) the physical unit is damaged by abuse and traumatized by violent life experiences and/or

b) the physical unit is taught to be afraid of spiritual realms.

To a certain extent of course we all experience damage and trauma, and of course, many of us are taught to be afraid of authentic spiritual connection.[116] But in some people the damage is extensive and the fears pervasive.[117] This damage and fear can undermine the ability of the physical unit to connect in a grounded and proper fashion with higher consciousness. In cases where damage is great and fears are deep and pervasive, connection can be resisted with great neurotic intensity. In the worst cases, connection can lead to the collapse of the bodily ego and the experience of acute, or even chronic, psychotic pathology.[118] It can be very bad indeed. Of course, it is important to note that these are not necessary outcomes. Even individuals who have experienced extensive damage can heal and prepare for the descent of Consciousness into the body. But, when the physical unit is damaged, **connection pathology**[119]

---

[115] Charles P. Heriot-Maitland, "Mysticism and Madness: Different Aspects of the Same Human Experience?," Mental Health, Religion & Culture 11.3 (2008). See also Mike Jackson and K.W.M. Fulford, "Spiritual Experience and Psychopathology," Philosophy, Psychiatry, & Psychology 4.1 (1997).

[116] We are scared with boogey-man tales of demons and devils, or told that mystical/experience and/or religious belief is an indication of stupidity and something only weak minded people have.

[117] My own experience with fear, which I outline in the chapter on the origins of the Lightning Path, is representative of some of the problems that may be encountered.

[118] I shall explore some of the pathologies of connection in Michael Sharp, The Book of Magic, vol. 1, 7 vols. (St Albert, Alberta: Lightning Path Press, unpublished).

[119] A connection pathology is a physical, emotional, psychological, or spiritual illness, usually arising as the result of

is a possibility. In order to ensure the best outcome of mystical connection is attained, problems have to be anticipated.

In this regard, the Lightning Path anticipates problems and helps prevent difficulty by providing a solid and grounded foundation for spiritual advancement. Part of this foundation for connection is the previous stipulation to recognize abuse, stop it, and heal the damage; but the LP goes way beyond that by providing concepts, practices, guidance, and an advanced spiritual psychology that provides a solid and safe platform from which to undertake spiritual exploration and reconnection. The concepts, practices, and guidance of the LP can make the difference between confusion, disorientation, and devastating madness, and the positive, salutatory, and beneficial outcomes so often associated with properly grounded mystical experience.

Providing Support

Finally, the sixth way the LP helps you on your way toward reconnection with the Fabric of Consciousness is that it provides a support framework. Support is important in a number of ways. We have already talked about the need for guidance through the chaff and detritus of modern spirituality, but supporting spiritual awakening and activation goes beyond mere guidance and direction. For one thing, mystical experiences can sometimes be challenging to understand and ground. Nature experiences, peak experiences, and brief glimpses of oneness and connection are positive, uplifting, and generally easy to deal with, but other forms of mystical experience can be powerful, provocative, and a major psychological and emotional challenge. For example, sometimes the implication of a mystical realization can be disconcerting. I know one student who called me up once in a

---

toxic socialization, that prevents an individual from seeking, maintaining, and/or establishing a proper, persistent, and healthy connection to Consciousness. http://www.thespiritwiki.com/Connection_Pathology

panic at the realization that everything existed in Consciousness and that if Consciousness disappeared, so would all of physical creation. This is certainly true, but only in theory. In practice the disappearance of God would require the disappearance of all of us and that is no more likely to happen than all the grains of sand on this Earth to suddenly disappear. And it is not just the profound implications that can be unsettling for some. It is not uncommon for an individual's entire world to be turned upside down by a moment of visionary or revelatory mystical experience. In the post traumatic hours, days, and even years following a powerful mystical experience, having someone to talk to and having qualitative, grounded, and trustworthy resources available to help and orient you, are essential. Support here can make the difference between a productive experience that keeps you moving toward more permanent reconnection and a traumatic event that turns you away from authentic spirituality altogether.

Beyond the powerful and visionary nature of some mystical experiences, there is also the issue of discipline. Having a single mystical experience is easy. Many people have single mystical experiences. But a single connection experience does not make for true salvation. *All a single mystical experience does is show you what you are missing.* A single mystical experience is like a post card from home, really. It is a teaser that makes you aware of the possibilities and a glimpse that encourages you to shift your focus and priorities. It is a tidbit designed to turn you onto the path and that is all. It is definitely <u>not</u> your final destination. Single mystical experiences show you the beauty, grandeur, and warm familiarity of spaces you once knew, but that's all. If you want to actually travel home, if you want to get back to the beauty and grandeur of higher consciousness, you have to walk the path, and that takes more than a single experience or two; that requires discipline and practice. If you want to permanently exist in higher levels of consciousness, you have to do the work. "Doing the work" is probably not what you think though. Doing the work doesn't mean rubbing singing bowls, tuning to crystals, or engaging in spiritualist prophecy. Doing the work means consistent use of mantras and intent and consistent effort to align your physical unit and your physical reality with the nature and expectations of your higher consciousness. Doing the work means establishing **right thought**,[120] creating **right environment**,[121] engaging in **right action**,[122] and remaining disciplined and focused. It is a lot of work and it is very easy to get distracted.

As noted, powerful visionary experiences and the hard work and discipline required to move forward can be challenging, and LP support can help with these challenges; but these are not the only challenges. A third challenge you face is the gargantuan nature of the task before you. As more of your higher consciousness seats itself in your physical unit, awareness will grow and you will become more and more aware of just how messed up this world, and perhaps your world, really is. The more aware you become of the problems that need to be fixed, the more overwhelmed you may become by the tasks that lie to hand. At the point where you begin to become overwhelmed, you may consciously or unconsciously turn away from spiritual practice. You may make a conscious or unconscious decision to stay within the box of "normal" and you may unconsciously allow yourself to be distracted.[123] Once again, this is where LP support comes into play. The LP

---

[120] Right thought is thinking and ideas that support spiritual awakening. Right thought is thought that supports the expansion of consciousness into the physical unit. See http://www.thespiritwiki.com/Right_Thought

[121] Right environment is an environment that supports, encourages, and facilitates the expansion of Consciousness into the body.

[122] Right action is action/behavior that supports connection (i.e. the expansion of consciousness into the physical unit). http://www.thespiritwiki.com/Right_Action

[123] It is an understatement to say that we live in a distracting world. Thirty years ago, I had a lot of private spaces where I could read, relax, recharge, rejuvenate, and reconnect. Twenty years ago, I probably had less than twelve television channels with only a handful of good shows. Ten years ago, I saw advertisements on billboards, in magazines, and televisions. Today, we have networked computers, a multichannel universe, smartphones, and constant connection. There are no boundaries anymore. Media companies can get at us wherever we are and the problem is just going to get worse. In this modern world of techno-wizardry there are no private spaces. Distractions come in fast and furious and in this cauldron of constant media bombardment it is very difficult to stay focused on something as ethereal and outside the box as authentic spiritual practice.

support system gives you the tools you need to stay on task, and puts you in touch with others who have gone through the process. You can discuss with them the sometimes overwhelming challenges you may face and this can help you stay motivated, disciplined, grounded, and pointed in the right direction.

More could be said about the importance and significance of good support, but I'm sure as your awareness of the obstacles and challenges along the path grows, you'll realize it for yourself. If you do find you need support, I keep a list of support options at http://www.thelightningpath.com/support/. As of this writing support options are slim, mostly just an online community at http://www.thelightningpath.com/forums/ and also a social media framework that helps keep you focused and on Path. This is just the beginning however. The LP is working toward the development of professional spiritual guides (LP Mentors) and a proper educational program aimed at training spiritually sophisticated healers, (psychologists, psychiatrists etc.). You can keep up to date on developments by visiting the website and signing up for the newsletter.

Origins

In the last couple of chapters of this book we have learned a bit about the Lightning Path, what it is, and what makes it unique and powerful. We learned that the purpose of Lightning Path spirituality, indeed the purpose of any authentic spirituality, is to lead you toward full time connection with The Fabric of Consciousness. I have to say, full time connection with The Fabric is not the easiest thing to do, at least while socialized and indoctrinated within The System. If it was easy to do we would live on a planet of accomplished mystics, but we clearly do not. For whatever reason you might want to give (and I give quite a few reasons throughout the Lightning Path corpus, like confusion, psychopathology, misdirection, doubt, disbelief, active suppression of our spirituality, etc.) most people are confined to minimal spiritual experiences, brief connections, or one-off mystical experiences. That is, most people may have a liminal feeling, a few peak experiences, an auditory or visual connection experience, and maybe a vision or two, but it never gets very far beyond that. People have their experiences and do enjoy improvements, sometimes slight, sometimes profound, in mental and spiritual well-being as a result, but by and large they all settle back into "normal" consciousness and normal routine. It is too bad. As Abraham Maslow recognized, "the world would be a much better place if we all embraced our inner mystic!"[124]

As you know, the Lightning Path is designed to correct this issue and make mystics of us all. Accomplishing this goal is no easy task. I know from my own personal experiences, from my observations of others, and from reading and analysis, that having a mystical experience is not always so easy and straightforward. This is especially true of full blown mystical

---

[124] A great statement of Maslow's position is provided in one of his last papers where he began to develop a "transhumanistic" psychology. See for example A. H. Maslow, "The Farther Reaches of Human Nature," Journal of Transpersonal Psychology 1.1 (1969).

connections. Minor mystical connections like peak experiences[125] and other (what I would call) **glimmerings** are not normally problematic.[126] In fact, even minor mystical experiences can be positively transformative, healing body and mind. But this isn't always the case with full blown mystical connections. A full blown mystical connection can be positive, life affirming, and transformative—what I call a **zenith experience**;[127] but it can also be dramatic, disorienting, and so discombobulating that it can blow your psychological and emotional circuits, what I call a **nadir experience**.[128] Because of the potential dangers, perusing a full blown mystical connection is not something you want to do without some form of preparation, and this is where the LP comes in. The LP is all about the preparation. The LP provides theoretical perspectives, archetypal revisions, and practical spiritual technique designed to help you reconnect with The Fabric in a safe and grounded fashion. The LP provides a foundation upon which to make the highest level connections possible.

At this point I cannot go into a lot of direct detail about the training involved or the spiritual content of the LP corpus. There is a lot of content and discussing it here would be a distraction from these introductory materials. Instead, allow me to continue this introductory corpus by speaking briefly about the origins of the LP. As we'll see below, the LP originates exclusively in my own powerful mystical experiences. It is these mystical experiences, all "initiated" one fateful day when I was 39 years old, which triggered the formation and development

---

[125] Abraham Maslow both defined, and had a lot to say about Peak Experiences. Maslow, Religions, Values, and Peak-Experiences, Maslow, "A Theory of Human Motivation.", Maslow, The Farther Reaches of Human Nature.

[126] For a typology of mystical connections, from glimmer to full blown vision, see http://www.thespiritwiki.com/Connection

[127] A zenith experience is any positively felt connection experience. http://www.thespiritwiki.com/Zenith_Experience

[128] A nadir experience is a negatively felt connection experience. Nadir experiences are unpleasant moments of stress, anxiety, anger, confusion, fear, paranoia, and even psychosis caused when Consciousness descends into a physical unit that is unprepared, damaged, or embedded in a toxic milieu. http://www.thespiritwiki.com/Nadir_Experience

of the Lightning Path. It is worthwhile knowing this story I think not only because it may be interesting as an example of the mystical awakening process, but also because it will illustrate some of the key concepts introduced (like the difference between zenith and nadir experiences) and some of the challenges involved. I suspect that not every detail of my experiences will be relevant to everyone (each path and process is idiosyncratic), but at the same time I think that there is considerable overlap in how we experience connection and awakening. As a result you, and even though you may not find every detail of my own process relevant, I'm sure you'll find something familiar and probably even helpful.

Mystical Experience

To be perfectly clear, I began writing Lighting Path materials in 2002 after a series of dramatic mystical experiences (what I would now conceptualize as crown and third eye chakra activations) "blew open" my head and led me to question my traditional spiritual skepticism and adopted scientific atheism. Although I did not understand what was happening at the time, I would say now that during those initial experiences I suffered spontaneous mystical connections with what I have come to call the Fabric of Consciousness (or what I would otherwise conceptualize as God with a big "G"[129]). The first opening occurred one night as I sat down to watch a movie entitled *The Abyss* with my wife. I sat down, the movie began, I had a very small puff of marijuana (the first time in decades), and suddenly I was confronted with none other than God the Almighty Patriarch, or at least what I perceived as God the Almighty Patriarch. One moment I was sitting watching a movie and the next moment I was streaming consciousness and having a full blown conversation with the God of my Christian background.

Now, you might expect, especially if you have read about other

---

[129] Sharp, The Book of Light: The Nature of God, the Structure of Consciousness, and the Universe within You.

peoples' mystical experiences, that I experienced wonder, glory, and joy in this initial contact with God; but I have to say, the connection experience wasn't pleasant at all. In fact, the experience was terrifying. For the first ten minutes of the film I engaged in a "dialogue with God"[130] whereby I confronted horrible fears of rejection, judgment, and damnation. Basically, I sat there on the couch gawking at the television, feeling that God was terribly disappointed in me, and terrified that God had arrived to judge me and cast me into the fiery pit of hell! I felt I was a sinner, a bad boy. I felt that I was unworthy of God's love. Honestly, I felt like a cosmic pile of turd. Indeed, I felt so unworthy of divine grace and God's Love that I thought that the only thing God wanted to do with me was throw me in a pit and burn me in hell for all eternity. I was transfixed by the terror. There I sat on a couch facing the abyss, fully expecting eternal damnation. I have to say, I was terrified and caught up in the heightened awareness brought on by the oxygen flow of Consciousness into my brain. The whole thing felt as real as a slap in the face. It is hard to convey the level of stress and trauma in these few words and I have really nothing else to compare it to so as to give you an idea of it. Let me just say, it was the most terrifying experience of my life. It was like I was a small child being confronted by a powerful parent who seemed intent on causing me eternal bodily harm. Terrifying, powerless, subjugated, defeated, worthless, useless, insignificant, inconsequential, and cosmic garbage are adjectives I could use to describe my feelings during this experience.

Interestingly enough, this was not the first time I had

---

[130] I put the phrase "dialogue with God" in scare quotes here because even though I thought I was engaged in a dialogue with God, even though I thought God was standing over me with a disapproving look and stern, judgmental hand, ready to pass me judgment and pass me off to his buddy Satan where I'd finish out the rest of eternity in pain, I wasn't engaged in a dialogue with God whatsoever. In fact, God wasn't talking at all during my traumatic experience, only I was. I was engaged in an internal monologue of anxiety and fear with the vision of God instilled by my Catholic indoctrination. God was pretty much silent through the whole thing, patiently waiting for me to smarten up and calm down. As you will see in the main text, God only started to talk a day or two after I had "broke the chains," after I settled down, and after I got my feet on the ground.

experienced this terrible fear of God. I had experienced it off and on as a teenager and young adult, usually (though not always) following a youthful experiment with marijuana, psilocybin, or LSD. The thing is though, I had thought I had overcome this spiritual trauma. You see, I was raised a fire and brimstone Catholic, but I left the faith when I was only eight years old and completely rejected it by the time I was twenty-five. The catalyst for my rejection of Catholicism was an event that occurred with my mom. One day, when I was about eight years old I was helping my mom in the kitchen. My mother was baking some cookies and I, anxious and inexperienced as I was, reached into a hot oven and grabbed the pan handle with my bare hand. I burned my hand severely and my mom, rather than comforting me with compassion and understanding, as parents should when their children experience pain, grabbed my hand, held it up to my face and exclaimed "hell will be much worse than this." Even though I was badly hurt and even though I was only eight, I could nevertheless see that something was terribly wrong with my mom and her beliefs. Even at eight I couldn't abide the psychological violence of a statement like that and so, blaming the Catholic Church for teaching my mom such hurtful nonsense, I left the faith. I did not totally give things up right away. I searched around a bit in my teen and early adult years looking at Theosophy, Eckankar, the (at the time) emerging New Age movement, Buddhism, Zen, and so on; but a lot of the writing was obtuse and confusing and nothing really satisfied, so I never committed to any one thing. Then one day I entered a university, took a Sociology course, and heard Karl Marx's infamous assessment of religion echoing through the hallways of scholarship and history.

Religion is the opiate of the masses,[131] said Karl.

"Ding, ding, ding" went my brain. "Of course, that was true," I thought to myself. Sociologists could see it all clearly! Religion

---

[131] Karl Marx, "The German Ideology," <u>The Marx-Engels Reader</u>, ed. R. Tucker (New York: Norton, 1978).

was an ideology that supported social control. Religion was a pacifier that prevented social change. Religion was the cause of my existential anguish and terror! That was it. That was the answer. Back then, I didn't have a lot of respect for religion and spirituality and so back then Marx's assessment made total sense to me. So, without further ado, I completely rejected spirituality, religion, and God as the ideological and infantile delusions of an oppressed and infantile planet. Subsequent to that, I did not want to have anything to do with God, religion, or spirituality. I focused on my studies, got my university degrees, and settled into a Sociological career. I was happy, satisfied, and sure the Catholic trauma had been healed. I knew the truth and the truth had set me free! I was proud of my accomplishment! I puffed up my chest and I ruffled my peacock feathers. Like many atheists, I was arrogant in my rejection of faith, sure of my superiority of perspective, and confident that I had resolved the trauma and abuse of my childhood religious indoctrination.[132] But as my traumatic mystical experience testified to, I was wrong, and for a time, confused. Given that I had rejected religion in favor of secular humanism a decade earlier, and given I knew with absolute certainty that we lived a material world, it didn't make any logical or intuitive sense for me to be confronting deep religious fears in my late thirties, much less talking directly to God, as came later. But, there it was. Deeply buried inside me just waiting to emerge full blown was a childhood fear of God. Who knew just how successful my mom had been at implanting the fears of the Church? Who knew that even as a forty-year-old scientist with twenty years of avowed atheism under his belt I could still be that frightened little boy with the burned hand, looking for acceptance and love, but getting only pain, abuse, and rejection in return. Who knew that there was more to life

---

[132] Actually, to be honest, during my years as an atheist I was totally oblivious to the depth and breadth of the trauma caused by the psychological, emotional, spiritual, and physical violence and abuse of my childhood. It was only later, as I thought about my mystical experiences and the difficulties I initially had with them that I realized just how damaged I really was.

than met my empirical eye? Certainly not me! As a scientist, it was all about what you could see. If it wasn't real in the material sense, if it wasn't part of the material universe, it wasn't real at all. But, what happened that night and in particular what followed shortly thereafter, had no empirical explanation at all. As I realized that night that *there was a lot more going on beneath the meniscus of this reality than I had previously thought.*

But, I'm jumping ahead. We should probably get back to the story of the Lightning Path. Recall, I sat down to watch a movie with my wife. Recall, I had a small toke (something I hadn't done in decades). Recall that suddenly God was standing before me. Recall the toxic monologue triggered by God's presence. Realize the terrible, immobilizing fear of God on display here. So what did I do? After sitting for a few minutes (minutes which honestly felt like an eternity) absorbed in the trauma of my own worthlessness, and waiting for God's cosmic hammer to fall, a little switch went off inside. Basically, I just got tired of the whole thing. I got tired of the fear; I got tired of the trauma; I got tired of the emotional anguish; I got tired of being made to feel like worthless cosmic turd; and, I got tired of sitting like some passive sheep just waiting for God to finally smack me down into the fire. I was tired, frustrated, and fed up so I "stood up,"[133] raised my fist in the air, gave God the middle finger, and said "fuck you and fuck off you horrible piece of creator shit."[134]

Oh, yes I did! I looked God square in the eye that night and I said to "him"[135] that if "his" idea of love and acceptance involved eternal fire for those children who didn't live up to his standards

---

[133] Just a point of clarification, I didn't really "stand up" to do to this. When I say that I stood up, I mean that in a metaphorical way. This monologue of fear all occurred in my head as I sat glassy eyed, staring at the television.

[134] I hope the reader will excuse the language, but these are the words I said and I believe it is important to recount the night's events just as they happened.

[135] I'm going to put gender pronouns in scare quotes here. I'm using the pronoun for literary effect here, but please realize that God has no gender at all, neither male nor female. Let me repeat. God, or what I call The Fabric of Consciousness, *has no gender at all.* Human bodies have gender, consciousness does not. We'll explore this unique feature of the LP (i.e. the removal of gender from the spiritual equation) throughout the course of the LP training.

and expectations, then "he" could take his pathetic idea of creation and fuck right off because I didn't want anything to do with it anymore. And if he wanted to throw me in hell for my insolence, fine. If everything I had been told about God the great and powerful was true, I was hooped and there was nothing I do about it anyway.

And so, there I was. I said it and then I sat back, took a few deep breaths and waited for the lightning bolt to strike me down. But, the lightning bolt never came, at least in the form that I was expecting, and so I watched the rest of the movie and then, still traumatized, went upstairs to bed.

The next day, I woke up mildly surprised that God hadn't killed me in my sleep. I scratched my head for a bit and tried to process. After my insolent outburst I was sure I was going to be dead, or worse. Surely if God did exist "he" would have done something about my brash disrespect. After decades of listening to organized (and not so organized) religions and their representatives rattle off about the violent, abusive, and fowl tempered God, I expected that "he" would never have stood for such an insolent outburst from such a worthless and pathetic soul. But God didn't do a darn thing! In fact, all I got was silence, and relief. God, if "he" had been there at all, didn't seem to be interested in my anxiety, fear, or profane outburst at all. God, if he did exist, clearly wasn't the abusive and violent patriarch that I had been told. Clearly, if God did exist, I had been lied to. But, whether God existed or not didn't matter at that point. The big thing for me was relief that my fears were unfounded. I mean, if God didn't smack me down after that outburst, clearly I had nothing to fear. After realizing that, my fear, for the most part, dissipated.[136] I told God to f-off and I was suddenly "clear." And that, dear reader, is where the fun began because after telling God to f-off something remarkable

---

[136] I say "for the most part" here because the truth is, I continued to process the "fear of God" (and some other fears) for some time after that, but it was residual. Once I realized that the fears that had been implanted by my Catholic indoctrination were unfounded, a little bit of intellectual effort was all that was needed to keep the fears in check. Eventually, the fears dissipated altogether.

happened. Just a couple of days after I uttered the fateful heresy, words began to flow out of me like water flows out of a fire hydrant. And it wasn't just a poem or two, or an article here and there. All of a sudden information was spilling out of my brain in a veritable gusher. All of a sudden, I was writing poems, parables, books, and creation stories about things I had barely thought of before.[137] The very first thing that came spewing from my brain was an epic poem that I called *The Song of Creation: The Story of Genesis*. This epic poem is a complete story of creation with some rather unique characteristics.[138] The Song covers the entire cosmic expanse from "the beginning" all the way to the "end-times" and beyond. I also wrote a poem called *Shambhala Warriors*,[139] a poem called *The Redemption*,[140] a parable entitled *The Parable of the Room*,[141] and I even got started on a book entitled *The Book of Life: Ascension and the Divine World Order*.[142] Remarkably, I did this all in a period of about a month. What is perhaps more remarkable is that it hasn't stopped. A decade and a half later, I still sit down every day and let it flow. The body of work that is slowly emerging is nothing less than remarkable, in my eyes anyway, and totally

---

[137] I should note that me making this claim is not unusual. Other mystics make the same claim from time to time. For example Madame Blavatsky, famous theosophical author of the two volume work *The Secret Doctrine,* and *Isis Unveiled*, said her mystical experiences gave her knowledge and information for things she had never studied. For more, see Alvin Boyd Kuhn, Theosophy: A Modern Revival of Ancient Wisdom (Phd Thesis) (Whitefish, Montana: Kessinger Publishing) 114.

[138] What is unique about the *Song of Creation?* One of its primary unique features is that it contains no duality. That is, there is no intimation of good versus evil, no suggestion that we are in some kind of cosmic battle, and no effort to draw boundaries and exclude. In *The Song* we are all shining members of a glorious family of spirit. Michael Sharp, The Song of Creation: The Story of Genesis (St. Albert: Lightning Path Press, 2006).

[139] http://www.michaelsharp.org/shambhala-warriors/

[140] http://www.michaelsharp.org/the-redemption/

[141] See Michael Michael Sharp, Parable of the Room, 2003, Available: http://www.michaelsharp.org/parable-of-the-room/, Feb 27 2014.

[142] See Sharp, The Song of Creation: The Story of Genesis., *The Song of Creation, Michael Sharp*, The Book of Life: Ascension and the Divine World Order *(St. Albert, AB: Lightning Path Press/Avatar Publications, 2003)., The Book of Life: Ascension and the Divine World Order.* For a couple of early poems, see Michael Sharp, I Am/We Are, 2003, Lightning Path Press, Available: http://www.michaelsharp.org/i-am-we-are/2014., *I Am/We Are* or Michael Sharp, Daughters of Isis, 2003, Lightning Path Press, Available: http://www.michaelsharp.org/daughters-of-isis/2014., *Daughters of Isis,* or Michael Sharp, Shambhala Warriors, 2003, Lightning Path Press, Available: http://www.michaelsharp.org/shambhala-warriors/2014., *Shambhala Warriors.*

without precedent, at least to me. It came out of the blue, so to speak, and gushed into the world through my little brain and my fast, touch-typing fingers. I still shake my head in surprise whenever I think about it.

Shock and Awe

I have to say, the whole thing was incredibly surprising. As it began to kick into really high gear I was in fact shocked and awed by the whole thing. One minute I was a scared little spiritual child and the next I was a conduit through which flowed the wisdom of spirit. It was a big surprise and a lot to take in for a few reasons. **For one thing**, the information flow was massive. It flowed from my fingertips page after page after page. I could barely keep up. It was a good thing I was a fast touch typist. Had I not been a touch typist, had I been confined to pen and papyrus, had I not had modern computer technology at my fingers, I would not have been able to get it all down in anything close to a complete sense. Under different circumstances I would have been able to capture only a small fraction of the breadth and detail. And that is remarkable because before I told God to f-off, I struggled to write. I could write, but it was laborious and painstaking. Now all of a sudden it was a painless gusher. It was like night and day really and honestly, at the time, I had no explanation for what this gusher was or why it was happening to me. Of course, now I know what happened and why. After over a decade of research and analysis I now know that the gusher happened after I cleared psychological and emotional blockages embedded in my little ego (fears, in this case) that prevented me from making a connection to Consciousness. Once those fears were cleared I was able to make a solid and persistent connection. Once connected I had access to the glorious Fabric of Consciousness, a Fabric so vast and so grand that the limited intellect of what I call the bodily ego is nothing but a dim candle flame. Once I had access to the vastness, it was a simple matter to open a channel and pipe massive amounts of information through. But I didn't know that at the time and in my ignorance and confusion I was shocked and awed by the munificent vastness of the flow.

If the massive information flow wasn't startling enough, the **second reason** it was all so astounding was because after I told God to f-off, my interests and abilities seemed to totally change. Before "it" happened I had never written a poem, parable, or non-academic book in my life; but afterwards, I was writing varied and copious spiritual works. Sure, I'd written academic papers before. In fact, I had a lot of experience doing that kind of thing; but that stuff was staid, boring, dry, and nothing like I am doing now. Before the experience I had never written anything more interesting than a scholarly journal article, but after the experience, I was suddenly a full-fledged mystic writing parables and poetry and even constructing my own set of archetype cards. The empirical reality is that *I went from an avowed atheist to a full-fledged artist and mystic in a little under two days.* It was a one hundred and eighty degree shift of interest, perspective, and talent and it occurred in the span of only a few hours. With minimal effort and no formal training I was off to the creative races. This "shift" was surprising in itself. What was more surprising was that to make the shift all I had to do was commit a grand heresy by telling God to f-off.

If the massive information flow and dramatic shift of perspective, talent, and interest were not enough, add to that the **third reason** for my surprise, which was the content of **The Stream.**[143] Before I gave God the finger I was thinking about learning objects, the labour process, and other sociological type topics; after I gave God the finger I was thinking about consciousness, creation, the end-times, the spiritual composition of the physical universe, chakras, kundalini, and

---

[143] The Stream of Consciousness is a term used to describe the random and/or directed flow of images, ideas, sounds, and silences that pass, like water flowing down a river, through your awareness. See http://www.thespiritwiki.com/Stream_of_Consciousness

so much more. Indeed, what I was thinking about after what I now call my clearing experience was a long way from the staid and boring stuff I had been working on previously. Following my experience, almost every thought that passed through my head had spiritual, cosmological, and even eschatological content. And to underline just how surprising that was, take *The Book of Light*[144] as an example. I started writing The Book of Light just a few weeks after my initial clearing experience. I sat down and literally had a conversation with God about the cosmos that (as I learned) we had all created. I connected with The Fabric, connected with God-level consciousness, and God reminded me why the universe was created and how it all unfolded. I know it sounds crazy, but that is exactly what happened. I sat, I listened, and God told me how it was.

You have to admit, this was (and I find still is) all very surprising, and perhaps a little unbelievable to many. The last thing you would expect to flow from the pen of an avowed atheist, one with graduate degrees from respectable universities, was a book chronicling a conversation with God about the divine nature of Consciousness and Creation; but, there it was. And here arises the **fourth reason** for being startled and surprised. One moment I was an avowed atheist and the next I was completely convinced in the spiritual world and the existence of God. One moment I thought God was a figment of somebody's over active imagination, and the next I knew God like I knew my name is Michael. I knew because I had a phenomenological / noetic experience that could not be denied. Right now, and in this moment you could no more convince me that the universe is a universe empty of Spirit than you could convince me that my name was Frank. Which is to say, you can't. You have to agree, that's quite the shift. One day I was a regular, run of the mill atheist and the next day I was a dyed in the wool mystic with a

---

[144] See Sharp, The Book of Light: The Nature of God, the Structure of Consciousness, and the Universe within You., *The Book of Light Volume One - Air* and Michael Sharp, The Book of Light: The Nature of God, the Structure of Consciousness, and the Universe within You, vol. two - water, 4 vols. (St. Albert, Alberta: Lightning Path Press, Unpublished)., *The Book of Light Volume Two - Water.*

personal relationship with God. One day I was minding my own business walking the hallways of my atheist university, the next day I was literally spewing words on a page. One day I couldn't care less if God existed, the next day I knew God with the same certainty that I know my name. Honestly, when I go over it all in my head, I'm still taken back by the sudden grandness of it all.

At this point you can probably understand the reason for my surprise. A gush of information, a shift in interest and abilities, a dramatic shift in thought patterns, and a fundamental revolution in belief systems left me scratching my head and asking WTF? Of course, this sort of fundamental revolution is quite common when people have mystical experiences, and it is something that I understand completely now; but it was a surprise to me at the time. As a scientist I had to ask myself the question, "What the heck had just happened?" What happened to turn me away from normal consciousness toward the deep mysticism that I have come to be so familiar with? Really, the only concrete thing that had happened is that I'd uttered a few hostile words in my head to a God that many would dismiss as a neurotically creative delusion. Telling God to f-off hardly seemed like a reasonable catalyst for full blown mystical comprehension of the universe, at least according to what I had been taught were requirements, yet there it was. The tiny little bit of cannabis that I had consumed that night seems insufficient to trigger such a visceral and terrifying experience. Obviously, something was going on here and that something needed to be explained.

To be (a mystic) or not to be (a mystic)

Answering the scientific questions that were raised by the process I underwent was something I'd have to do eventually; but honestly, scholarly analysis did not concern me too much in the beginning. In the beginning, my primary concerns were a) resolving the cognitive dissonance caused by the experiences and b) deciding whether or not I should continue. It was a problem on both fronts. As for resolving the cognitive dissonance, recall I had adopted scientific atheism as my creed at an early age and up until my mystical experiences I was quite confident in the veracity of this perspective. My mystical connection experiences challenged my atheist worldview and required me to either a) reject my own experience as delusion or b) rapidly evolve my perspective and position so that it could account for my experience. Considering that the new mystical perspective was diametrically opposed to the old atheist perspective, this process of evolution was not without challenge. Suffice it to say here that I eventually resolved the dissonance by dropping my atheist perspective. I now know atheism to be a scientifically invalid perspective, incapable of explaining both my experiences and the spiritual realities that lie just underneath the thin meniscus of our normal reality.[145]

A bigger and deeper problem than resolving cognitive dissonance however was deciding whether or not to continue with the whole affair at all. As I noted above, the spiritual clearing that I had accomplished brought with it copious information flow. There was very real pressure to write it all down and share it with the world. I had no illusions about that at all. As soon as I completed the *Song of Creation* I knew this was something that was intended to be shared. But did I really want to do that and, more importantly, what would that involve? I had overcome a deep set of fears and had opened to a universe of mystical experience that I had not known existed, but I was not sure if I should continue. I had to think long and hard about whether I wanted to pursue the mystical vistas before me, or whether I wanted to return to normal consciousness and live there like everybody else. Although I

---

[145] For a rundown of some of the reasons I feel atheism is invalid, see Mike Sosteric, "Mysticism, Consciousness, Death," Journal of Consciousness Exploration and Research 7.11 (2016).

eventually decided to move forward with mystical adventure, this was not a given. I had to think about and overcome additional fears before I could tentatively, much less comfortably, adopt and move forward in my new role.

Fear One: My "Normal" life.

The first fear I had to overcome before I was comfortable moving forward was my "normal" life. Even though a spiritual earthquake had recently destroyed the foundation of my "normal" life and existence, and even though the aftershocks were still rumbling through the fabric of my being, I had a good job, a career, colleagues, and a family that knew me a certain way. I wasn't prepared to abandon/leave that all behind, but I thought I might have to. Initially I thought abandoning my "normal" life and going to "hold the light" on a mountain top away from all the people might be an expectation, even a job requirement. I had picked up the thought from somewhere,[146] and there are examples of academics that had experienced magical connections to consciousness and subsequently abandoned all to pursue their mystical core.[147] Indeed, over the years I have met more than a few people flying a banner of spiritual enlightenment but totally oblivious and unconcerned regarding their responsibilities to spouse and child. I could see people abandoning their lives in one way or another and I thought that I might need to become some sort of spiritual hermit to do the job that I now seemed primed to do. But I had

---

[146] At the time I did not know why I thought I had to abandon my life, or where I got the idea. Later on, and in particular as I analyzed the masonic tarot, I realized that the idea is part of a collection of ideas/archetypes designed to control and contain spiritual awakening experience, to make sure most people don't have the transformative/revolutionary experiences that lead to better connection. This particular archetype, the "hermit" archetype we might call it, suggested that to be truly spiritual you had to live an isolated existence. Obviously if you believe this archetype, it limits who can participate. Those with full time jobs, those with family responsibilities, and those who want a life are automatically excluded from spiritual attainment.

[147] The infamous example here is Richard Alpert who had some LSD experiences, gained "enlightenment," changed his name to Ram Dass, and moved off to sunny California to spread his prophet seed. Who knows who, or what, he abandoned on his pursuit of spiritual "grace." Another example is a sociologist by the name of Edward Carpenter who abandoned his career to go work on the land Anon, "Edward Carpenter: Red, Green and Gay," Socialism Today 131 (2009), Sheila Rowbotham, Edward Carpenter: A Life of Liberty and Love (New York: Verso, 2008).

no desire to abandon anything or anybody. To my mind such an action seemed grossly irresponsible and solipsistic; and frankly, I was happy where I was. Therefore, I knew from the start that if I moved forward it would have to be in the context of my current life, with my current family, and in my current job. The question for me at the time was, could I do it? Could the two be successfully blended? The answer, fifteen years later, is an unreserved yes; but, at the time I wasn't so sure and I worried what might become of me. Obviously, I did decide to move forward; but, I was cautious and careful as I did.

Fear Two: Professional Censure

A second fear that caused me to pause and consider whether moving forward was a good idea or not was the possibility that if I moved forward and suddenly declared my mystical transformation, I would be professionally censured. In the early days, fear of repercussion/persecution was a problem. What would my colleagues think? What would my friends think? Would I be laughed out of the academy? Would people think I was crazy? Would I be excommunicated from science for my views? These might sound irrational and unfounded to some, but they are valid fears. As the story of Rupert Sheldrake reveals,[148] scientists have indeed been excommunicated for stepping too far outside the establishment's box.

As a sociologist, this felt like a particular problem for me because sociology can be quite hostile towards religion in general, much less mystical and religious experience in particular. Sociology's hostility arises from "separatist principles" adopted by sociology's founding elders.[149] These principles have led subsequent generations of sociologists, to accept, present, and expect, sociology to be religion's

---

[148] Freeman, "The Sense of Being Glared At: What Is It Like to Be a Heretic?."

[149] Steven F. Cohn and Kyriacos C. Markides, "Religion and Spiritual Experience: Revisiting Key Assumptions in Sociology," International Journal of Transpersonal Studies 32.2 (2013).

executioner. Sociologists felt that sociology, as a science, would disprove the claims of religion and help establish human knowledge upon material foundations.[150] These "separatist aspirations" are especially prevalent in sociological luminaries who have rejected spirituality as elite machination,[151] cussed stupidity,[152] and implausible and superstitious nonsense likely to die out as secularization tromped its way through the unfolding history of modernity.[153] When minds as great as Mark and Spencer cry foul, only a fool does not sit up to listen.

The whole separatist agenda is formalized in what sociologists call the secularization thesis.[154] This thesis holds that religion would eventually die out as society modernized and industrialized, and as people got smarter and less superstitious. Of course, religion hasn't just disappeared in a puff of secular smoke. In fact, spirituality and religion of one sort or another continue to be relevant to the vast majority of people on this planet, but what the masses think and believe was no consequence to me at the time. It matters not that the secularization thesis has proven to be absolutely wrong, or at least not as straightforward as first imagined, hostility towards religion, especially in sociology, is palpable and severe. I didn't want to risk professional censure and I certainly didn't want to lose my job; so, I definitely had to consider the possible consequences before moving forward at all.

---

[150] Cohn and Markides, "Religion and Spiritual Experience: Revisiting Key Assumptions in Sociology."

[151] Peter Berger, The Sacred Canopy: Elements of a Sociological Theory of Religion (New York: Anchor Books, 1969).

See also Marx, "The German Ideology."

[152] Berger, The Sacred Canopy: Elements of a Sociological Theory of Religion 4.

[153] Steve Bruce, God Is Dead: Secularization in the West (Oxford: Blackwell, 2002).

Also see Karel Dobbelaere, "Trend Report: Secularization: A Multi-Dimensional Concept," Current Sociology 29.2 (1981).

Peter Berger, A Bleak Outlook Is Seen for Religion, vol. April 25 (The New York Times, 1968).

[154] Emile Durkheim, The Elementary Forms of Religious Life (New York: Free Press, 1965 (1912)), Durkheim, The Elementary Forms of Religious Life.

Fear Three: The Unknown

Besides my anchor in normal life, and the fear of professional censure, another reason not to continue was the weirdness of it all. And I have to say, it was weird. Nothing I had ever read in the areas of religion or science had ever prepared me for the thing that happened when I cleared the blockage. There was no precedent; it was strange, strange, strange; much stranger than I am prepared to go into here. At the time, there was a lot I didn't know about the experience or why I was having it. I had some intimations, but frankly some of those scared me. Even at the start I felt that there was something vast, even revolutionary, here. It was only days into the journey and already my ideas of God, Earth, human nature, and teleological purpose had been transformed. Even now, if I pause to think about it, it can seem overwhelming. Couple the stupendous and revolutionary nature of it with the fact that I was on my own and you can perhaps understand my reticence. Nobody around me, and nobody I had ever read, had anything useful to say about what was going on. I even thought I might be mad. There is, after all, a long association of mysticism with madness, and with what was happening to me I thought I might be walking the razor's edge. I went from isolated and cut off to channeling mystical madman in the space of only a few days. I have to admit, it was a bit scary. In those early days I could have easily put it all down to illusion, delusion, and maybe even psychosis and just walked away out of fear and self-preservation. As you know I didn't, but I could have.

'Tis Nobler to Suffer

My anchor in normal life, my fear of professional censure, and a concern with the odd/unknown nature of my experiences led me to doubt my own experiences and question whether I should move forward. Obviously, since I am writing this book and you are reading these words, I overcame my fear and doubt and moved forward into mystical exploration. It is going on fifteen years now since I first initiated down this path and I have no desire to do anything but continue. Indeed, my passion and resolve are stronger than ever. As I gradually meld the science with the spirituality, I am more certain every day. But I wasn't at the time. At the time I had to carefully consider and evaluate, and that I did. I spent a lot of time thinking about what I was doing and asking myself the question, "Should I continue?" Eventually, as you know, I decided to keep moving. But even so, I was careful. Because of the issues mentioned here, and because of a few I haven't bothered to recount, I didn't fully commit right out of the gate. As it is for many I suspect, it wasn't an all or none decision, which is to say, I struggled. The process of acceptance has spanned more than a decade of uncertainty and self-doubt, but I didn't let the doubt and uncertainty stop me. The uncertainty has gradually transformed into resolve, and the self-doubt has gradually transformed into confidence. And now, here I am. I suppose a question that might now arise is, why was I able to keep moving forward?

Under Control

One of the first reasons I chose to continue and not just shut it all down was because the process seemed to be under my control. To be sure, some of the information that flowed in the beginning did stretch the boundaries of credibility and materialist common sense; but even so, I wasn't having an ongoing and uncontrolled (or, as the misinformed might say, psychotic) conversation with God, nor did I have a significant break with reality. I opened the connection when I wanted it open and I shut it down when I didn't. Except for a few fear based hiccups in the beginning, hiccups that diminished over time as I reminded myself about the truths I had learned, it was very much a smooth and grounded process. There was nothing of the uncontrolled delusionary outpourings that are sometimes associated with mystical experiences, at least to my mind. Certainly some of the information that came through was extremely unconventional, even bizarre; and sure, as we will see in the next chapter, there were problems; but these were manageable. I seemed sane, I acted sane, I could still live my life and do my job, and any bizarre things could be carefully boxed in and grounded over the long term. I felt I could keep both worlds sufficiently separate to avoid any negative outcomes (like professional censure or excommunication), so I didn't think the exploration would be a problem. Of course, I did take steps to protect myself. As already noted, sociology in particular, and academics in general, can be hostile to spiritual experience. As irrational and unlikely as it might seem to some, I didn't want to go the way of Rupert Sheldrake. Therefore, I decided to keep my spiritual and academic identities separate. I did this by writing my spiritual stuff under a pen name, Michael Sharp. This way I could avoid any unwanted scrutiny before I was ready to "come out," so to speak. With that, I felt comfortable moving forward, and so I did.

Scientifically Fascinating

The second reason I didn't just throw up my hands and walk away was the material that was coming through, and the process that seemed to be involved, was too fascinating to simply ignore and walk away from. It was fascinating at a number of levels. For one, the information that was flowing was voluminous. Information spewed out on the page like water spewing from a fire hydrant. It was a veritable pressure gusher, and by that I mean I literally felt pressure to get all the information out. And that was, frankly, startling. I had never experienced anything like it before. I did find out many years later, while reading a book called *Mystics* by Harmless, that copious output is a defining characteristic of the professional mystic's work, but long before I knew that this was "normal" I found it quite fascinating. I knew there was something here that needed to be explained and although I was pretty sure I knew what it was all about right from the start, I also knew I had my work cut out for me if I was going to make academic sense of it all.

And note, that copious mystical spew wasn't the only fascinating thing about it all. I was also fascinated (and startled) by the fact that *the information that came through was way beyond what I had learned in my time here on this Earth.* The information that was finding a channel through me was not what I would have reasonably expected to know, especially if I was relying on just my material brain, neurology, and this-life experience. Had the information been coming from me, I might have expected Christian style information based on the sort of things I had learned in church as a child, or scientific style ruminations based on my scientific training, but I didn't get that. What I got was information that was totally novel to my frame of reference, and totally beyond my reasonable expectations. To be as clear as possible, I was learning stuff that I had never been taught in school, church, or university. I even came to understand later that I was learning things that other people hadn't written down before, particularly around notions of archetypes and spiritual indoctrination. Indeed, in some cases what I got was so beyond my prior religious and scientific training that it was total heresy!

Such is the case with the *Song of Creation: The Story of Genesis*. This "song" is an epic poem, a creation story, that leaves behind standard spiritual conventions (what I would call old energy conventions) and develops a **New Energy**[155] narrative and **New Energy Archetypes**.[156] In this story, I don't talk about fallen angels, good and evil, judgment, or the mistakes that we have all made. In this story, I don't talk about chosen ones, God's wrath, or the punishment we can expect to receive. In this story I leave behind retributive notions of karma and judgment and I elevate humanity above the status of ascending evolutionary ape. In the song, I present a novel statement of spiritual purpose that, unlike so many other canonical statements of spiritual purpose, unites and empowers humanity

---

[155] Energy that is balanced (equal yang/force and yin/formation. New energy is both outgoing/generative and receptive/formative, in equal amounts. See http://www.thespiritwiki.com/New_Energy

[156] New energy archetypes are archetypes whose creative intent is the awakening, activation, and ascension of the planet. See http://www.thespiritwiki.com/New_Energy_Archetypes

rather than divides and inhibits. It is a totally novel creation story with a completely new energy purpose. But that's a story for another place. The point here is simple: copious flow and novel information tweaked my professional curiosity.

I have to say, copious information flow and ongoing mystical and scientific heresy were not the only fascinating things about the process. A final fascinating feature of the mystical flow was that much of the information came out fully formed. I didn't have to think about it at all![157] *In an instant I knew and understood everything*, even if that "everything" was a total violation of all I had known before. In a series of what can only be called dramatic mystical revelations, I knew about God, I knew about Consciousness, and I could see the entire vista of physical creation stretched out in an enlightened tapestry before me. Of course, even though the material was fully formed, I did think long and hard about the material, and I did have to work with it (i.e. edit, revise, etc.) to work it up into acceptable form. I had to. It might have been divine revelation, but as we will see in the chapter on problems, there were issues with the information and these issues had to be addressed. Nevertheless, the copious, unexpected, and visionary quality of the information kept me focused on moving forward, even while firmly embedded in the flow.

A Sociologist's Loving Touch

Speaking of problems with the information flow brings us to the **third reason** why I decided to stick with it rather than return back to normal. It became clear at a very early stage that the area of mystical/religious experience badly needed a sociologist's touch; and by that I don't mean that the area needed a sociologist to look at it and analyze it, because a few sociologists have done that before me. By that I meant that the

---

[157] Well, this is not quite true. As we'll see in a moment, even though some of the information did come to me fully formed, this information was not always in a form recognizable to my white, Western, mind. Some of it was clearly from another culture, to say the least. Information like that had to be grounded and processed to make it sensible/palatable to Earthlings, and less confusing/disorienting to my mind.

area needed a sociologist to dive in and investigate, in an ethnographic/participant/sympathetic sort of way, the whole experience of mystical connection. A sociologist needed to become a mystic and to explore the cosmic hallways of mystical experience. A sociologist had to "go native," so to speak, to get a better idea of what was going on inside this phenomenon of mystical/religious experience. It is not that unusual. "Going native" is something that sociologists, like anthropologists, do from time to time. Indeed, we've been doing it at least since the Chicago School of Sociology made qualitative research and participant observation (à la Bronislaw Malinowski and Frank Boaz) a valid research method for sociologists.

Of course, the question at this point is, why go native in relation to mysticism? The reason is simple. Participant observation is a powerful research method that provides a window into phenomenon not possible with more quantitative research methods. I don't want to distract you by going into an analysis of the strengths and benefits of participant observation in relation to mystical exploration at this time. Here I'll just say that participant observation gives you depth and breadth of analysis, the ability to penetrate deep into a phenomenon or area of interest, and the power to develop unique perspectives not possible when pursuing phenomenon in a laboratory or in a quantitative fashion (i.e. with survey and numbers). As I am fond of repeating, traditionally, sociologists have looked at the institutional side of spiritualty and little more. Getting involved with mysticism as an embedded participant would allow me to shine a badly needed light on mystical phenomenon in a way that no sociologist had done before.

Just how badly the area needed a sociologists touch is, I believe, demonstrated by a 2014 article I wrote entitled *The Sociology of Tarot*.[158] That article examines the tarot (which is a common

---

[158] Sosteric, "A Sociology of Tarot."

spiritual appliance[159] in New Age, pagan, and sometimes even traditional Christian households) in a way that only a sociologist could. That article exposes the tarot, which has been used without much critical thought by people for over two centuries now, as a masonic elite penetration into the spiritual lives of the people of this planet. That article traces the history of the modern occult tarot directly to the emerging Freemason lodges of revolutionary 18th century Europe and shows how high level Freemasons used the tarot as a vehicle for developing and delivering spiritual thought control[160] aimed at shaping and controlling the behavior of elites, and quieting and controlling the revolutionary populations of Europe. That article is important because it:

a) exposes the true purpose of Freemasonry, which is to manipulate and control the population.

b) reveals the true nature of the Masonic tarot as a powerful ideological tool.

Any sociologist reading these words will recognize the key sociological significance of the tarot. Like the media it is an ideological tool used to manipulate and control the masses. It is not the most influential ideological tool, but it is a significant one. Decker, Depaulis, and Dummett, this world's foremost authorities on tarot, call the sum total of tarot activity engaged in by cleric, priests, and Freemasons in the 18th century the:

> ...most successful propaganda campaign ever launched: not by a very long way the most important, but the most completely successful. An entire false history, and false interpretation, of the Tarot pack was concocted by the occultists; and it is all but universally believed" [161]

---

[159] A spiritual appliance is an item useful for facilitating Connection and, consequently, awakening, activation, and/or ascension. See http://www.thespiritwiki.com/Spiritual_Appliance

[160] If you are uncomfortable with the idea of thought control, use the weaker term "propaganda."

[161] Ronald Decker, Thierry Depaulis and Michael Dummett, A Wicked Pack of Cards: The Origins of the Occult Tarot (New York: St Martin's Press, 1996) 27..

What is remarkable about the tarot is that it has taken so long for sociology to see the tarot as a significant topic of interest. And note, it is not just the tarot that needs attention. The tarot deck is just one aspect of a range of spiritual phenomenon, totally ignored by sociologists, but that carry social class, power, hegemonic, and other sociological implications. From careful examination of the *Secret Doctrine,* to analysis of mystical experience, to looking at the social class of channeling, to digging out the racism and elitism of some modern New Age authors, there are any of a number of sociological relevant spiritual phenomenon that need to be addressed, but that haven't been because only one or two sociologists have ever presented mysticism, esoteric materials, and spiritual experience in anything other than a derisive and dismissive light.

As a mystic, I know this dismissal of mysticism, esotericism, and spiritual experience is unfair. Even if one discounts the spiritual validity of mystical experience, there is still a lot of sociological relevant content to explore. That there is sociologically relevant content is, as I have already noted, one of the reasons why I decided to stay on to explore. The area needs more sociologists. It would be a disservice to the discipline, and to humanity, to just scoff and walk away.

A Mystics Critical Glare

I will have more to say about the process of mystical experience, participant observation, and the significance of sociological interest in said phenomenon at a later date, but hopefully I have at least given an indication of why I decided to make mystical experience a subject of a participant study. The area needs sociological attention. However, it is not just mystical and spiritual experience that needs attention. There are some issues with science's approach to mystical experience as well. These issues, which hamper investigation and understanding, become apparent when viewing science from the perspective of the mystic. If science is going to move its understanding forward, these issues have to be addressed.

The first issue that becomes apparent when we cast a critical glare at science and its treatment of mysticism and religious experience is that scientists can be a bit arrogant, especially when it comes to questions of God, consciousness, and mystical experience. Scientists can have very strong opinions. They can be insulting to those who don't talk in the expected fashion or agree with the accepted scientific cannon. This insulting arrogance can be accompanied with what can look a lot like religious fundamentalism at times, with scientists acting like their science can do no wrong, defending their science as if it is "the truth and nothing but," and deriding those who don't have their materialist beliefs. Richard Dawkins is a case in point, and probably the worst example of scientific arrogance,[162] but other examples could be cited.

The righteous arrogance of some scientists would be less of a problem if they actually had something useful to say, but they often don't. Scientists who adopt an arrogant stance towards human spirituality often focus narrowly on what I call **Church God.** Church God refers to the patriarchal personification of God offered to the masses by priests of Western ecclesiastical institutions. Church God is a sexist, racist, and classist construct that reflects the sexist, racist, and classist men who use it to a) control the thinking and behavior of the masses and b) use it to justify wealth and privilege. Atheist and scientists tend to reject Church God outright, and for good reason. But they don't go any further than that. They assume Church God is the only conception of God/Consciousness there is (it is not), they generalize this conception to all human spiritualties (i.e. they assume that all spiritual people must believe in personified deities), and they reject human spirituality outright. As a result, they never take a closer look and they never have anything useful to say about the more complex and nuanced

---

[162] Richard Dawkins, The God Delusion (New York: Mariner Books, 2006).

understanding of God found outside of the narrow purview of Western exoteric ecclesiastical institutions.

Not all scientists prejudicially reject all human spirituality based on an overgeneralization of Church God. Many scientists believe in something, and some (more than you might realize) actually find evidence for God in nature; but rarely does this belief amount to much of anything at all. This is particularly true of western scientists who haven't gotten any closer to a theorization/representation of God than Albert Einstein. Albert Einstein clearly believed in God. Of course, this wasn't the Church God of western institutions, it was more of a **Science God** of vast and complex intelligence.[163] But like the atheists who overgeneralize Church God, Albert didn't have much of anything to say on the topic. All Albert had to say on the issue of Nature God was that man [sic], with his limited intelligence, would never be able to understand it. Nature God was just too much for little old humanity to grasp. The best humanity could hope for would be some basic appreciation for the creator of all things. Beyond that, Nature God was a mystery. This is pretty bad. On issues of God/Consciousness, Science either rejects human spirituality outright or cops out.[164] It doesn't have anything to say about a fundamental aspect of human experience, spirituality.

Of course, I am being a little harsh here. Some scientists do investigate human spirituality. Psychology has a long history of looking at religion and religious/mystical experience, and sociology has a long history of looking at the institution of religion. But even there, the understanding of the depth and

---

[163] For a discussion of Einstein's spiritual beliefs, see my Sharp, <u>The Rocket Scientists' Guide to Money and the Economy: Accumulation and Debt.</u>

[164] This cop out still occurs. For example, physicist Edward Witten recently *said*

I think consciousness will remain a mystery.... I tend to think that the workings of the conscious brain will be elucidated to a large extent. Biologists and perhaps physicists will understand much better how the brain works. But why something that we call consciousness goes with those workings, I think that will remain mysterious. I have a much easier time imagining how we understand the Big Bang than I have imagining how we can understand consciousness.

breadth of human spirituality can be thin, vacuous, limited, and full of prejudice. Sociology is a case in point. It looks at religion and cult phenomenon but totally ignores mystical experience.[165] As sociology has itself admitted, sociology's dismissal of mystical experience has left their understanding of human spirituality a poorly drawn caricature, or as Bourque (151) charges, "highly stylized" and "simplistic…"

I totally understand why science, especially in the West here, avoids discussion of God and tends to hold religious experience at arm's length. The history of the Western Churches, the erstwhile carriers of canonical discussions of God and spirit, are nefarious. From crusades to inquisitions, the assassination of "heretics" to the attempt to suppress an emerging science, the Western Church clearly had, and still has, issues. Add to all that the fact that the Western Church is clearly an ideological arm of the ruling class and you can see why most scientists would want to avoid it, and whatever it talks about, like a plague. Spiritual discussions have been tainted as a result of their cooptation by ecclesiastical institutions. The Church talked about God, therefore God is clearly a fiction. The Church speaks about Jesus and mystics, therefore that is clearly bullshit. But, while I can understand why scientists avoid discussions of God and mystical experience because I did it myself at one time, now I don't condone the avoidance. Now I feel scientists really need to look at it. If Einstein hadn't copped out, if he had been more of a role model in this regard, if instead of saying "I dunno," if he had decided to devote some of that vast intellectual energy of his to the study of God/Consciousness, if he had explored phenomenologically, if he travelled the dark continent, could you imagine what he might have said, what we might have learned, and where we would be today? Could you imagine where we might be now in our understanding of things mystic and divine? Einstein wrote a couple of physics papers when he was but a child; can you imagine what he might have

---

[165] Mike Sosteric, The Sociology of Mysticism, ISA eSymposium for Sociology.

done if he focused his attention on mystical experience? Wow! The world would be a much better place now.

Anyway, it is not my intent here to cry over spilled milk, nor is it my intent to point fingers. The point here is to make the case that scientists need to pay closer attention to god, consciousness, and mystical experience. Except for a couple of notable exceptions, scientists haven't really treated it with the care and respect it deserves. That's unfortunate because as a mystic looking in on how science treats God, consciousness, and mystical experience, I have to say, I'm very disappointed in science. There are a lot of fascinating things to discover. It is a virtually untapped area. And, if you ask me, figuring it out is how science can help save the world. If science would stop dismissing this important aspect of human experience and just *do the job they are paid to do,* which is to find out the truth of things, maybe we (and by "we" I mean the human race) might stand a chance.

If you are a scientist looking in and I've convinced you of the need to take a closer look, the question now becomes, how to do that? That's where the value of being a mystic comes in because as a mystic I have to say that if you want to understand God, Consciousness, and mystical experience, then just like the original anthropologists who travelled to native societies in order to explore, observe, and discover, you are going to have to travel to mystical realms and engage in a bit of scholarly exploration. You don't have to spend years exploring, writing, and analyzing as I have done, but you do have to at least visit.

Why?

Because if you don't, anything you say will be narrow, thin, and caricatured. As a mystic I have to say, if you don't go exploring for yourself, then you'll be one of those blindfolded scientists feeling up an elephant, pretending to know, but at best only offering the clumsy observations of a sightless old man. If that sounds harsh, what can I say? It is true. I am not the first mystic to say if you want to know, you have to do.

Of course, the billion dollar question now is, how do you do. Well, as it turns out, exploration is not that hard. Even better, there are some tried and true methods for engaging in that exploration without ever leaving the comfort of your favorite chair! I won't go into the details here. If you want to jump ahead of the curriculum, check out my article *The Science of Ascension: Bodily Ego, Consciousness, Connection.*[166] I will say this though, as a mystic who has explored the "dark continent" of Consciousness for over a decade now, my message to science and scientists is that there is no other way. If you are a scientist interested in studying mystical experience or learning about God, the only way to get beyond prejudice and misconception, the only way to step out of your materialist arrogance, the only way to truly understand, is to explore for yourself.

And that is the LP origin story. To summarize, the LP originated in a series of mystical experiences which rocked my world. When I had the original experiences I had a decision to make. I could either move forward and explore or return to normal consciousness. Despite some early doubts and disbeliefs, despite some challenges (many of which we will discuss next chapter), and despite the possibility of professional censure, I decided to move forward. I had no reason not to. I had control of the process and I was generating some fascinating insight. Not only that, as I progressed I gradually realized that both science and mysticism could use the unique perspective brought about by my "dual citizenship" (i.e. scientist and mystic). The highly transformative potential inherent in a sociologically grounded mysticism,[167] the fact that Sociologists have paid almost no attention to mystical or religious experience in the past, and the fact that science clearly needed a better perspective pretty much sealed the deal. I knew

---

[166] Sosteric, The Science of Ascension: Bodily Ego, Consciousness, Connection.

[167] For the transformative potential of mystical experience, see my article, Sosteric, Dangerous Memories: Slavery, Mysticism, and Transformation.

I had to continue and so that is what I did.

The outcome of my decision to soldier on is a growing body of work with the ostensible goals of bringing science to mysticism, mysticism to science, and the planet to full connection. If the truth be told, it is a body of work intended to revolutionize our science and our spirituality. It is a body of work that embraces both science and spirituality, both God and Darwin if you like. Whether or not these goals are reasonable and achievable is an open question, but these are all questions that I want to ask.

Some Challenges

As noted in the last chapter, the Lightning path is rooted in my own effusive mystical experiences. As also noted in the last chapter, these mystical experiences were fascinating and challenging. It was the fascinating nature of the phenomenon and my growing realization how important it was for sociologists and for mystics to have a modern say that kept me moving forward with the experience and the scholarly analysis. I did have to struggle a bit with doubts and disbeliefs early on, but I did move on, and that is where it got really interesting. As I gradually learned to blast the spigot full on, and as I began to grind it all down, I gradually came to realize that having a mystical experience and dealing with the personal, psychological, emotional, familial, social, economic, and even political fallout was not as unproblematic as some people might like to believe. It wasn't just an issue of gush it all out, write it all down, have a talk with Oprah, and teach. There was a lot going on and I struggled to sort it all out and make something pure and true. I struggled to deal with the expansion of consciousness. I struggled to understand and accept. I struggled moving towards the new reality made possible by revelation and realization. I even struggled with my own brutally damaged bodily ego. I can tell you now that while the arrival may be glorious, the journey is as hard as hell.

I don't want to bore you with all the nitty gory details of all the challenges I have faced. We all have different histories, we all have different purposes, and we all have unique challenges. My struggles and challenges are not necessarily your struggles and challenges, nor are they bigger, better, or more significant. They are just my challenges. Still, you may be able to learn something about the challenges you will face by learning something about the challenges I have faced, and still face. You may also learn something about the nature and significance of the LP. Since I'm sure you're interested in how to overcome your own challenges, and since this book is, after all, an introduction to the LP, I'd like to spend some time going over some of the challenges I faced with a view towards a) educating you so you can understand, b) helping you so you can overcome your own challenges, and c) further revealing the core of the LP.

Effusive Flow

I have to say that one of the first challenges that I had to face in regards to mystical experience was effusive flow. In my initial mystical experiences information came through fast and furious. When I sat down to explore the hallways of consciousness, the stream that flowed was like water gushing through a fire hose, which is to say, there was lots of it, and it flowed under very high pressure. Of course, as a scholar I had written things before; but, as a scholar the process was always slow and laborious. This was something else altogether. While operating in mystical mode the information gushed.

This effusive flow presented me with a couple of complex challenges right out of the gate. The first challenge I faced was getting all the information down fast enough so I wouldn't forget the details as it came through. This was a big challenge, especially in the beginning where it was very much like sitting in a room and listening to a bunch of people talk at the same time. There was so much information and the information pushed so hard to get out that it was all I could do to simply get it all down. Poems, parables, books, how-to articles, and so on spewed from my pen at an astonishing rate.

So, how did I do it? How did I get it all down? Really, the only reason I was able to get it all down, the only reason I was able to do it on my own without scribes and apostles and others to help was because I had a computer and I was a fast touch typist (upwards of 80 words a minute last time I checked). It sounds ridiculous, even absurd to make such a claim, but it is true. Without modern computer word-processing there is no way I would have been able to meet the challenge of the effusive flow.

That is, I wouldn't have been able to get it all down much less work it into a pure and transformative whole, as was my goal right from the start. Advanced transcription and editing technology was key.[168] To get it done right, we really needed the technology of advanced Capitalism.[169]

Of course, a computer and touch typing are not the only reasons I was able to handle the flow and get it all down. I also needed safety, a comfortable house, enough food to eat, a supportive/nurturing environment, and enough time to accomplish it all. If I had to beg for food, if I didn't have a safe and comfortable home, if I had to wander in the desert or work day, if I didn't have a good day job, I wouldn't have been able to do what I came to do. And that is saying a lot. Two thousand years ago, perhaps even as recent as 50 years ago, it would have simply been impossible to process and present the exuberant flow that comes from connection in anything like a reasonable way. I would have been too busy surviving or fighting, or simply not fast enough to get it all down. Now I have the technology and the conditions that I need to handle the effusive flow and get the job done.

Unformed Lumps

Still, even now, even in the ideal conditions of my technological and academic world, even though I can handle the effusive flow, there are still challenges. For example, even once it is all down, it still takes time to understand the flow and process the information to a point where it is of useful and useable nature.

---

[168] In other words, it is only been in the last twenty years or so that technology has been in a place where it could support our collective mystical/eschatological goals! This is something worth thinking about, especially when you think about past spiritual masters, like Jesus Christ, Mohammed, Sri Aurobindo, and others. The technology for success simply wasn't available to them.

[169] At this point you might ask, if we needed the advanced technology of capitalism to get it done right, why so many great spiritual teachers of the past? If we knew we needed to wait until technology developed, why send so many before? The answer is simple: we needed the practice. Just having the technology available isn't enough. You need somebody with the training, skill, and experience to use it just right. As any standup comic will be able to tell you, you only get the training, skill, and experience you need to be successful in one way, by actually going out and doing it in the real world.

Having the technology and life conditions necessary doesn't resolve all the challenges. This mystical spew that plops onto the page requires a lot of work to get into a presentable and powerful form, far more than I originally realized. When I first started I thought I could spew it all on the page, engage in a bit of revision, and be done with it. The information was all out in the gush, as it were, and I felt that it just required some finessing. As it turns out, that thinking was naïve. Although I did get a number of resources out in the first few years, these require ongoing work. Each work itself requires a depth and breadth of understanding that is only developed over time, and the entire corpus itself must work together. When it is flopped down on paper it is really just an unformed visionary/revelatory lump. As such, it needs a lot of work.

A good way to think about this is to think of a potter sitting before a spinning potter's wheel. The clay is down, the wheel is turning, and the potter may know exactly what kind of pot she wants to make, but in order to manifest her vision, before the lump is transformed into a beautiful pot expressing the potter's vision, the lump requires sustained attention and repeated effort. It is the same with the information that flows via my authentic spiritual connection. It often comes out in lumps and it often takes a lot of work to shape into a successful manifestation of the driving vision.[170] The only difference between me and the potter is that instead of working with one wheel and one lump, I am working with many wheels and many lumps simultaneously. If I am to achieve my goal, if I am to manifest the vision of global transformation and global unity through the LP corpus, all these lumps need to be carefully formed and precisely presented, otherwise you end up with a useless pedagogical/spiritual/literary mess.[171] It is a lot of work,

---

[170] Which is, in the case of the LP, global unity and global transformation.

[171] Just look at something like the *Sophia of Jesus Christ* or the *Sepher Yetzirah* and you'll see by their confused and confusing state that sculpting work is obviously required.

but somebody has to do it.[172]

I cannot underestimate the need for me to shape and form the material as it comes through, especially since my goal is to teach others. I also cannot underestimate the amount of work involved in forming the lumpy clay blobs into something reasonably presentable. It was an obvious challenge for me and I hesitated a bit in the beginning. "Could I really do this?" "Would I have the time?" I have to admit, if I knew how much work it was going to be when I started, I might have chosen not to move forward with it at all. The things that got me going were the things I have already discussed, like the fascinating nature of the phenomenon, the clear need I saw for better perspectives and analysis, and so on. Later, by the time I finally realized just how much work it would be, there was really no turning back.

A Passive Receptacle

Dealing with the effusive flow, getting it all down, and shaping it into an acceptable form, were certainly key challenges, but another challenge, another beasty, reared its ugly head early on and this was the beasty of passivity. When I got started with the whole process, and for quite a few months after that, I had the feeling, reinforced by others, that whatever I did to get out the lumps of clay, once they were out I should just plop them down and leave them as relatively unformed lumps. I know that sounds bizarre, especially when using a pottery metaphor to describe the process. I mean, what potter would think it acceptable to just plop clay down in a lump and sell it like that! What consumer would accept a raw lump of clay? But, as

---

[172] Well that's not quite true. You don't have to do it. If your goal is just personal realization, i.e. individual awakening, activation, and ascension, you can generally settle for whatever visionary insights flow to you. You may have to do a bit of work to ground and process, but you don't have to engage in the effort required to work up the lumps into presentable wholes. However, if your goal is to communicate spiritual Truth to others, then you have a responsibility to do the work. You don't have to be a PhD sociologist to do it, though as we'll see shortly that can help, but you do have to put in the time and the critical effort. If you do not do the work then you run the risk of presenting inadequate materials and even leading people astray; and from a karmic perspective, you don't want to do that. It is one thing for you to be wandering blindfolded and lost in the desert by yourself, it is quite another thing to lead others astray with you.

bizarre as it sounds, that's what I was told. In the area of mystical religious experience there is a belief that when it comes to noetic revelation the mystic / priest / guru / avatar / messenger / apostle should just spew it down and leave it in its original lumpy form.

I know it sounds ridiculous, but it is true. We, and by "we" I mean just about everybody, think that when it comes to spiritual/mystical/Divine information, we are supposed to just stand there and receive the "higher wisdom." It is, after all, God's revelation. It is something to be inscribed on stone tablets and passed down untouched. And lest you think it is only the masses of the world who believe this, consider the scientist Dossey. Dossey provides a startling expression of passivity in the face of the Divine.

> There are no sure-fire formulas for loosening of the brain's filter function. Even when props and aids are used, as with Merrell and Yeats, access remains what it always has been—a matter of being, not doing. One sets an intention, then ushers the conscious mind out of the way. That is why the most spectacular manifestations of the overcoming of the brain's restrictions—revelations, epiphanies, creativity, discovery—occur when the discursive, striving, rational mind has been bypassed through reverie, meditation, dreams, or some other nonactivity. Muscular, aggressive, ego-oriented approaches do not work. Selfish entry—trying to access a higher intelligence in order to get something—is akin to burglary. Alarms get triggered, and the delivery system shuts down. One approaches the higher dimensions respectfully, acknowledging a source of wisdom and intelligence greater than one's own. One then waits patiently, and is grateful for what is given. [173]

---

[173] Larry Dossey, "The Brain as Filter: On Removing the Stuffing from the Keyhole," Explore: The Journal of Science and Healing 8.6: 320.

Note, it is possible to muscle your way into mystical experience, so Dossey is incorrect about that as well. Simply suppress the Default Mode Network in the brain. For more information on how to suppress the DMN network in

All I can say is, gag. Dossey is a scientist and scientists are trained to take an active role towards knowledge acquisition. Scientists never take anything at face value, or passively sit back and receive. Scientists explore, analyze, and research. That is what they do. So why does Dossey recommend we bend over and simply accept an intelligence "greater than our own?" Like I, he probably picked up the notion from a book or maybe a colleague. Maybe he talked to a priest or hierophant who told him that it would be a sacrilege to take an active, formative, role towards presumably divine information. Maybe he talked to a **double-N mystic**[174] who, awed by the powerful and **noetic**[175] nature of the vision streams, said leave it alone and don't touch it. Maybe he himself had a mystical vision and was so blown away that he dropped to his knees to pray. Whatever it was doesn't matter. What matters is that we a) recognize him taking this passive role and b) question the advisability of this passivity. I know I did. When I started the process I was advised to take a passive role. Like Dossey, I originally thought I should leave it alone and pass it through un-interfered with. I had heard priests and hierophants admonish against taking an active role and talked to quite a few double-N mystics who said "leave the lumps alone" and who actually got upset when I suggested that maybe we shouldn't be so passive and accepting. But my passivity didn't last long. I thought about it for a while, but I just couldn't do it. I couldn't just let it come through and leave it unformed. Even though some might proclaim a heresy,[176] I had

---

the brain, see Sosteric, The Science of Ascension: Bodily Ego, Consciousness, Connection.

[174] A Double-N mystic is a mystic who is both *novice* (i.e. new to the process of connection) and *naive*/ignorant of the social-class, political, and economic realities of this planet. Double-N mystics tend to respond to the power and the glory of the noetic stream by taking a subservient, passive role towards the stream. For more see http://www.thespiritwiki.com/Double_N_Mystic

[175] Noesis refers to the feeling that the information transmitted through a mystical connection is special and even privileged in some way. When people experience this they tend to elevate the information to a special ontological status superior to information they have received from other, less divine, sources. And who can blame them? In some cases it is the literal Word of God, and it feels just like that. It is, connecting with Reality with a capital "R". It is powerful and glorious, sacred, awesome, and pure.

[176] And some did, proclaim a heresy that is. I remember trying to explain what I was doing to one woman. When she found out I was actually vetting, editing, and analyzing what was coming through, she was horrified. She told

to edit and vet.

So what changed my mind? What made me put aside passivity and do the work? A combination of factors really. I believe it was

> a) Part temperament. I never liked the idea of passively accepting divine wisdom.
>
> b) Part past life experience. This is related to temperament. I believe I trained for this job for several lifetimes and that this training gave me the knowledge, expertise, and strength necessary to approach the material in a certain critical and professional fashion.
>
> c) Part scientific training, and in particular my training as a sociologist. As a scientist I had a hard time stomaching the notion that I should just accept divine revelation. As a sociologist, I recognized ideology in the stream right away.

All these things primed me and prompted me to take an active role, although I have to say, if there was any factor that was particularly important it was my training as a sociologist. In fact, to be honest, I believe my training as a sociologist was critical. I believe that if I had picked any other discipline to get advanced training in, I wouldn't be doing what I am doing today in the way that I have chosen to do it. It is because of the particular intellectual skill set of a trained PhD sociologist, and in particular the sociologist's skill at perceiving and unpacking ideology, that was key to overcoming passivity. Indeed, if there is one thing a sociologist is trained to see it is ideology. A sociologist can spot ideology a mile away. I know I certainly did. Almost as soon as I started I saw the ideology in the mystical stream. When I took a closer look, I could see clearly that the

---

me I should get my hands off and warned me I was engaging in a major spiritual sin (a scientist would say epistemological sin) and that I would be punished (by God I assume) if I didn't stop. It took me aback, I have to admit.

spirituality of this planet was soaked in it. From talk show "O" to pulpit priest, from New Age self-help author to sad, sad guru, ideology was there in the stream and corrupting the lumps of clay. As soon as I saw it I knew something was wrong. As soon as I saw it I knew I couldn't just let it pass through.

Ideology

So what is this ideology I speak of? Well, as any sociologist will tell you, *ideology is a collection of biased ideas and ideals designed to promote a particular political or economic agenda.* Ideology is basically sophisticated sales talk. Ideology sells you a particular view on the world without letting you know the possible detractions. The ideology of Capitalism or Socialism are examples. People who espouse either often talk up the benefits and downplay, ignore, or even lie about the detractions.

You should know, ideology can go beyond mere sales talk. True, an ideologue[177] can straight sell you something, but that's not always the best way to approach things. When you are aware that an ideologue is trying to sell you something, you are on guard against the sale. In its most sophisticated forms, ideology sells you a particular world view, perspective, or even car not by selling the individual view or item, but by selling you the components of the view. A good example of this would be a car salesmen trying to sell you a hot red Mustang convertible. A skilled salesmen won't sell you the actual individual car, he'll sell you the "fast ride," or the cool feeling, or the hot women you'll get with it. Selling you by using this **lateral ideology**[178] is a much better way to sell you a car or an economic system,

---

[177] An ideologue is someone who communicates ideology. An ideologue is like an unethical used car salesmen who sells you a rotten car without letting you know it has some issues. There might be some good things about the car you drive, but he hides the bad so you don't question the sale.

[178] Lateral ideology is indirect ideology. Indoctrination via lateral ideology occurs surreptitiously via sophisticated intellectual and emotional associations. For example, Christmas is a lateral ideology of capitalism and consumerism. For more, see http://www.thespiritwiki.com/Lateral_ideology

because when you buy the lateral ideology and then buy the car, you think you are the one who has made the decision. Lateral ideology obscure the ideologues action and makes you feel that you have made an independent (i.e. not manipulated) decision.

As I quickly saw in the beginning, ideology is definitely present in the spirituality of this world, so much so that I give it a special name. I call ideology present in the mystical streams/religious institutions of this world **spiritual ideology**.[179] Spiritual ideology is the same as ideology (i.e. it is a collection of biased ideas and ideals designed to promote a particular political or economic agenda), but using spiritual ideas to help support The System instead. From the Catholic Church's representation of God as capitalist authority figure, to certain Hindu scriptures which speak about the caste nature of reality as a reflection of the natural reality in heaven, to "guru" Ram Dass who justifies wealth by using a spiritualized form of liberal individualism, to Zeitgeist technophilia that pegs the solution to the global crises on more technology, the elites have been pimping spiritual ideology and corrupting spiritual truth from before the time of Christ.[180]

As already noted, as a trained sociologist I saw the presence of ideology in the mystical stream right away. As soon as I saw that, I knew I had to take a more critical look, and I did. From my training in sociology, I already knew there was ideology in church teachings; but I also found ideology in New Age and New Thought, in Western Tarot cards, in secret "spiritual" lodges, and pretty much everywhere else I looked. For

---

[179] Spiritual Ideology is a collection of spiritual ideas, archetypes, and spiritual ideals designed specifically to promote and support particular economic or political agendas. Spiritual ideologies function by providing justifications and excuses for the inequality, oppression classicism, sexism, racism, and homophobia that often attend a specific Regime of Accumulation.

http://www.thespiritwiki.com/Spiritual_Ideology. See also http://www.thespiritwiki.com/Regime_of_Accumulation

[180] There is, I believe, an entire social class history, yet to be written, of how the elites destroyed libraries, occluded texts, added and/or deleted words and phrases from canonical scripture, created ideological resources, assassinated world teachers, and even tortured and burned heretics (i.e. people who saw through their lies) in order to ensure they had control of the Word.

example, consider the Western tarot. The tarot is a 78 card picture deck with Italian origins.[181] Most people think of the tarot as just a deck of cards with antique pictures. Some people think of it as a spiritual tool. Others use it for divination. Of course, humans are creative and they can use a deck of cards for whatever they want to use it for, but as I found out, the creators of the "spiritual" tarot never intended it to be used for divination or spiritual advancement. They intended it to be used as an ideological tool for indoctrinating people. I know this might sound outrageous to some, especially those who are convinced the "mystical" tarot is a tool of archetypal or spiritual progress, but it is true. As I explored the tarot both mystically and scientifically I came to trace its origins to Freemasons lodges in 18th and 19th century Europe. There I found the tarot was recreated as an ideological tool of social control![182] As I noted earlier, freemasons created the tarot first to control their own members, and then to control the mass population. In order to do that they basically made things up about the tarot cards. They then transferred their made up ideas onto the imaginative cards of the Italian tarot deck. Then, they sold the ideological vehicle (i.e. the tarot cards) as if it was ancient spiritual wisdom sourced from ancient spiritual giants.[183]

I speak more about the tarot as spiritual ideology in my *Book of the Triumph of Spirit* series,[184] so I don't want to spend any more time on it here. I would like to say that the tarot is not the only "spiritual" place where spiritual ideology may be found. As I have gradually become more mystically and scientifically aware I have come to see clearly that ideology has penetrated

---

[181] Michael Dummett, The Game of Tarot (London: Duckwork, 1980).

[182] Sosteric, "A Sociology of Tarot."

[183] For a brilliant and insightful overview of the history of Tarot, see both Ronald Decker and Michael Dummett, A History of the Occult Tarot, 1870-1970 (London: Duckworth, 2002), Decker, Depaulis and Dummett, A Wicked Pack of Cards: The Origins of the Occult Tarot.

[184] Sharp, The Book of the Triumph of Spirit: Halo/Sharp New Energy Archetypes, Sharp, The Book of the Triumph of Spirit: Master Key, Sharp, The Book of Triumph of Spirit: Healing and Activating with the Halo/Sharp System.

everywhere into the spiritual discourse on this planet.

To summarize, when I began the process I had the idea that I shouldn't touch "sacred" mystical transmissions. Then, I saw ideology and I took a closer look. When I took a closer look, I saw the ubiquitous presence of spiritual ideology. The closer I looked, the more I realized that a) the infiltration was far worse than I had first conceived and b) sorting it out would be a lot harder than I originally imagined. Indeed, the presence of spiritual ideology in the mystical (and not so mystical) streams of this planet made my job as mystical potter a hundred times harder. It was like sitting at a pottery wheel for ten back-breaking days only to suddenly find the clay you have been working on is full of garbage and dirt. It's an emotional and intellectual catastrophe.

What do you do when you come to this realization? What do you do when you realize the spiritual systems of this world have been infiltrated? What do you do when you realize the work you've done and the time you have already devoted is only the very start? Well, you either give up or you soldier on. If you give up then, whatever... but if you soldier on,[185] then you only have two choices to choose from, and honestly, neither of them are very pleasant. You can stick with the clay you've already got on the wheel and try to salvage the work you've already done by picking the dirt and garbage out of the clay, or you can throw it all away and start anew. A committed potter could make either work, though neither choice is ideal. Both of these choices are difficult and involve a lot of work. Both require an environment conducive to the reset. Both require a long term commitment.

So what did I do? When I saw just how much dirt and garbage there was, I threw it all out and started anew.[186] I started,

---

[185] In your quest to understand, or your path to become a soldier of Truth...

[186] Other "potters" might disagree. Others might think it is possible to pick out the dirt and the garbage from the clay and fix it. Personally, I don't think so. I think the lump is too messed up and I think it is impossible to totally

formally, to create the Lightning Path which is, as you will see, a totally new lump of clay. The Lightning Path is a major spiritual rewrite, a total global revision, of the spiritual fabric of this planet. Instead of trying to preserve the work that's already been done, I chose to start anew. I have to say, it has been a challenge. I have had to provide new foundations,[187] a complete set of new concepts and ideas that we can use to think about and understand human spirituality,[188] new books and resources, new techniques of connection, and new spiritual appliances.[189] What's more, I've had to tie it all together with educational curriculum.[190] That's a lot of work. If you asked, I'd have to say I am about 60% through. It is slow, but I am making progress.

Of course, while it is true that dealing with spiritual ideology is a challenge, you, the reader, don't have to do the same amount of work that I have done. If I do my job properly, i.e. if I am successful at reworking the lump of clay, you can use the work I have done to reduce the amount of work you have to do and accelerate your progress dramatically. Still, having said that I still have to say, it's a lot of work, especially when it comes to getting over passivity and clearing ideology. You can't just sit down and allow me to feed you information. Whether you are learning from me or exploring your own mystical connection stream, you have to take an active role. You have to realize everything you read is not purely divine. More to the point, *you have to learn to recognize for yourself elite activity in the mystical streams of this planet.* I can't cover it all. It is impossible. I can only provide a beginning. I can only provide

---

clean out the dirty clay. I think it would take more time and effort than starting fresh, and even when the potter was done reworking the clay, she still wouldn't have an acceptable product. I think starting fresh is the only way forward.

[187] For example, my *Song of Creation* provides a new story of genesis that does not center around obedience, subservience, punishment, banishment, and (most importantly) does not, like all old energy creation stories, pimp conflict and war as something sanctioned by the cosmos.

[188] My SpiritWiki is the canonical glossary of Lightning Path concepts. See http://www.thespiritwiki.com

[189] For example, the Halo/Sharp tarot is one.

[190] Like the book you are reading now.

a fresh foundation. Unless you want to totally drop all your old global traditions and move forward with just the LP, you are going to dig around your own traditions and clean those out for yourself. And I have to say, even with the new concepts and ideas that I provide, this can be a lot of work, and it can be harder than you think. Even erudite scholars can miss it.

A case in point is Ehrman, who points out how the whole Christian idea that the Jews killed Jesus was an elaborate anti-Semitic hoax constructed over the course of several centuries of elite activity in the Church. His analysis is fascinating and compelling and could easily lead one to conclude that the elites of the Church and State colluded together to use Jews as a scapegoat for their assassination of Christ. But he doesn't. When he gets to the point where he asks himself the question, "so if the Jews didn't kill Jesus, who did," he doesn't mention the elite priests and Pharisees who were threatened by Christ and he doesn't mention Pontius Pilate the Roman authority figure who issued the assassination order. Despite the fact that he himself marshalled the evidence that leads directly to the conclusion that the history of Christ's death is a history of subterfuge and assassination, he doesn't state it. He just says God did it! Ehrman marshals all the evidence required to expose elite machination, but then in a massive display of sociological naiveté, totally misses the point.

This sociological naiveté is on display in full glory when he deals with the fact that the books of the New Testament were selected by elites. That is, political and ecumenical elites got together and decided what textual accounts would count as gospel, and what books Christians should read. Elite interference with scripture culminated when the elites, headed up by the powerful bishop of Alexandria, stamped Christian orthodox canon at **Synod of Hippo**.[191] That is, the bishop of Alexandria and a bunch of rich authority figures picked several books

---

[191] Bart D. Ehrman, <u>Misquoting Jesus: The Story Behind Who Changed the Bible and Why</u> (Harper One, 2007).

written about Jesus, called them gospels, and said *this is what you should read!* The Church subsequently destroyed other available texts,[192] continued to edit and revise remaining texts, and most curiously, restricted mass access to the books they had selected for over a thousand years.[193] That is, even though the elites of the Church had handpicked the books that the masses could read, they still felt the masses shouldn't read them! So, they locked them up and wouldn't give anybody but their priests access. They even went so far as to burn those who tried to put the bible into the hands of the people. Starr summarizes.

> Throughout the Middle Ages the Church went to great extremes to keep the Bible out of the hands of common people. Typical of prohibitions issues by the Church is the edit from the Council of Tarragona in 1234 that 'ordered all vernacular versions to be brought to the Bishop to be burned.' The 1408 Constitution of Oxford, England, strictly forbade the translation of the Bible in the native tongue. These restrictions were in line with a long tradition in Christianity of banning translations in native languages that extended into the sixteenth century and beyond. The ban on translations effectively took the Bible away from the populace, since few, if any commoners, could read Latin." [194]

When Starr tries to explain all this he misses elite activity. Instead of saying "rich patriarchs created the bible so they could control what the masses read," and instead of saying "they edited the bible to support their own agenda," he says "...Christians agreed concerning which books should compromise their sacred scripture..."[195] The problem with this

---

[192] Darrell L. Bock, The Missing Gospels: Unearthing the Truth Behind Alternative Christianities (Nashville, Tennessee: Thomas Nelson, 2006).

[193] Bernard Starr, Jesus Uncensored: Restoring the Authentic Jew (OmniHouse Publishing, 2013), Ehrman, Misquoting Jesus: The Story Behind Who Changed the Bible and Why.

[194] Starr, Jesus Uncensored: Restoring the Authentic Jew 162.

[195] Bart D. Ehrman, Lost Scriptures (New Yok: Oxford University Press, 2003) 1.

statement, other than the fact that it does not explain why Christians would burn other Christians for trying to distribute a book they had all "agreed" was worth reading in the first place, is that Christians as a whole didn't agree. As Starr himself clearly admits, Christians were largely illiterate during the day. They could no more make a decision on what books to include in the bible than I, an individual who knows no Russian, could make a decision on what chapters a Russian editor should put in a Russian chemistry text. It was the literate elites that selected the books that would be presented to Christians down through the ages.[196] Christians, on the whole, had no clue what was going on.

Finally, it wasn't just the fact that elites selected the texts that people could read, they also edited the books they did choose! Ehrman admits there are hundreds of thousands of edits in Church scripture. Ehrman glosses over the edits by suggesting that the ongoing elite modification of scriptures was largely undertaken with "good will," meaning they didn't do it for any nefarious reasons. But given the history of the Catholic Church, its burning of heretics, its violent crusades, and its clear representation of elite interests, such an assumption seems

---

[196] Why would they do such a bizarre thing? They did this, in my view, in order to remove the uncomfortably revolutionary implications of Christ's teachings. I explore the revolutionary implications of mystical teachings in Sosteric, Dangerous Memories: Slavery, Mysticism, and Transformation.

Just as a side note, allow me to say, I'm not standing in judgment of the elites. True they suppressed authentic spirituality to serve their own venal interests, but they did it not because they are evil. They did it because it is in their social nature. It is what they do. It is what we all do. We all elevate our group. I mean, you have to know, humans are not evolved from individualized predators wandering ancient African Savannas. Humans are chimpanzees who learned that if they wanted to survive the predators, they had to hang out in groups—which is what they did! The chimps that hung out in groups, the chimps that protected their groups, survived longer and had more children than the chimps who did not. The human physical unit is thus naturally selected to be social, and social animals naturally elevate group interests! It is what we do. It is what families do. It is what rich people do. It is what poor people do. It is what monarchists do. It is what socialists do. It is what Sikhs do. It is what Jews do. It is what Christians do. It is what rock bands do. It is what every single self-respecting social group you'd care to dream up would do. It is not evil, it is evolution. It's not Satan, it's a natural thing. It's a survival thing. Of course, the cosmic irony is that these days we live in a globalized world characterized by proliferating weapons, toxins, and pathology. These days, the activities of a single powerful group of greedy chimpanzees can wipe out all life on this planet, including their own. These days we can no longer afford to identify with groups. These days, that kind of primitive thinking will get us all killed. So, we either get beyond our primitive social programming and unite as a single global group of humans so we can join "the Federation" or we (as a species) die a long, slow, painful, and annoying, avoidable, death.

untenable and hopelessly naive. It seems more likely, or at least arguable, that the Church was protecting the interests of the elites and finessing its ideology[197] in order to obscure the revolutionary potential of Christ's teachings.[198]

Anyway, the long detour here is to illustrate a point, and the point is that even though I aim to provide you a lot of the groundwork, there is still a lot of work to do, especially with regards to unpacking spiritual ideology. There is a lot to do at a scholarly level to be sure, but there's also a lot to do at an individual level. Reading about it is not enough. You have to dig it out of your own spiritual traditions and you have to excise it from your own minds. If you don't do that, you don't move forward.

Intellectual Challenges

Effusive flow, passivity, and dealing with ideology were very big challenges, especially in the beginning. These were (and are) not the only challenges. Another very big challenge that presented itself very early on was the intellectual challenge of sorting out and grounding what I can only say is advanced (usually spiritual) knowledge. The intellectual challenge is multifold. How to process, ground, and discuss this information in a sensible, scholarly way is one intellectual challenge. How to deal with the challenge of canonical world views and established understandings of reality is another challenge. The information didn't always fit with what I had been told by parents, priests, and professors. Worse than that,

---

[197] It only takes a word or punctuation change here and there to totally alter the meaning of a text! For example, consider the dramatic difference between the sentence "Let's eat grandpa" and the sentence "Let's eat, grandpa." One portrays a cannibalistic world where the young feast on the old, while the other conveys a social world where the young respect and care for the old. Same words, one comma, different reality.

[198] Some readers may be uncomfortable with the notion that the Church does not represent God/Connection on Earth, but nevertheless this is a valid hypothesis worth considering. If true, it would explain why the Church fiddled with the texts for thousands of years, why they kept the bible they created from the people, and why they burned those who tried to distribute the text.

the information that did come through was often revolutionary (with a capital "R"). To say that my previous conceptions of life, the universe, and everything were off before these challenging noetic revelations would be an understatement of biblical proportions. It was difficult, and still can be difficult, to process, collate, and ground that revolutionary information in a sensible, non-triggering way. It's a big challenge, that's for sure.

I imagine it wouldn't have been so much of a challenge if there were established intellectual and conceptual structures that I could have used to understand what was going on, but there wasn't. I found quite early on that I couldn't use the dominant materialist paradigm that I had adopted as part of my academic training, because that just didn't fit the facts, much less explain them. Nor could I communicate in traditional spiritual terms. I knew the basic concepts and ideas of Christianity, Buddhism, New Age/New Thought, Hinduism, and so on(I'd been exposed to them all at an early age), but it was all so confused and confusing that I just couldn't figure it out. Even early on in the wake up process I knew there was something not quite right in ancient and modern traditions, something that I just couldn't fit my thinking process into.

So what did I do to handle the challenge? Well, before I even knew what was going on, I knew I had to build something new. I knew that if I wanted to be able to properly understand and eventually communicate the basic (and sometimes not so basic) noetic truths I was coming to understand, I would have to, from the ground up, rebuild the intellectual edifice. So, that is what I did. Or rather, that is what I am doing. I am laying the foundation,[199] building the scaffold,[200] and laying the bricks[201] necessary for a new and (as we shall see) syncretic global spirituality. That's a lot of work, and a big claim, but I think it's necessary. Without a new foundation there is no moving forward. It is just too much of a muddled mess.

This is a big intellectual challenge that's for sure, and I'll have more to say about the intellectual challenges, especially in regards to syncretism, in a few moments; before we get into that however, a few words about the emotional, psychological, and behavioural challenges I (really we all, to one extent or another) face are in order.

Emotional, Psychological, and Behavioral Challenges

Building an intellectual edifice capable of properly containing and communicating mystical noetic insights received during connection sessions is no easy intellectual task, but neither are the emotional and psychological challenges that come with connection easy either. Peak experiences and one off psychedelic trips are one thing, but full, direct, and persistent connection can strain even a healthy ego and body. Connection, and in particular persistent connection, is especially a concern for those whose egos are damaged by toxic

---

[199] The foundation is laid out in my SpiritWiki. The SpiritWiki

a) lists all LP concepts, both original and redefined
b) lists the books that the concepts are found in
c) provides theoretical notes to help expand our understanding of consciousness and creation (and also to expand consciousness), and
d) provides interlinking to related LP concepts.

[200] The scaffolding that ties it all together can be found in the **Master Map** I am developing. The master map is a mind map that links all LP topics into an interlinked representation that exposes and highlights concepts and their relation to each other. For more see http://www.thespiritwiki.com/Master_Map

[201] Finally, the bricks are the individual books and resources that introduce and elaborate the concepts and ideas.

childhood socialization, as mine was. Put a healthy bodily ego in contact with The Fabric and it can be a challenge. Put the psychologically and emotionally challenged ego of your average damaged and indoctrinated "normal" person in touch with the full force of the Fabric, and sparks can fly. Go one step further and put a severely emotionally, psychologically, verbally, and physically damaged bodily ego in touch with the Fabric and disaster can unfold.[202] In these situations the ego can a) blow up like the proverbial puffer fish, (b) deflate like a pin stuck balloon, or even (c) become disordered and schizophrenic.[203] When personality structures are severely damaged by the violence and toxicity of abusive environments, total pathology can result.

I have to admit, this was an issue for me. I would like to say that I was loved and nurtured as a child and that when I connected that love and acceptance made it easy for me, but I wasn't, and it didn't. I was subjected to physical, emotional, psychological, and spiritual assault at the hands of teachers, students, priests, and my own mother. All the toxic abuse that I experienced damaged my young ego, trashed my self-esteem, and instilled deep religious fears/misconceptions that at first prevented me from connecting and then, after a connection was made, threatened to undermine my ego and corrupt the information.

---

[202] This disaster has been called spiritual emergency by Stanislav Grof and Christina Grof, Spiritual Emergency: When Personal Transformation Becomes a Crises (New York: Putnam, 1989). I actually don't think that's the best name. That's like saying about an emergency patient that they have a medical emergency. It is true, but not very descriptive. A better term to describe what most people would see as a spiritual emergency is **ego explosion.** An ego explosion is a temporary or permanent collapse of the Bodily Ego, usually occurring as the result of a temporarily enhanced Connection to Consciousness. Ego explosion occurs when an unprepared individual makes (intentional or unintentional) contact with The Fabric of Consciousness. When that happens, the Light goes on. When the Light goes on, sparks can fly. If the sparks contact the combustible material of fear, trauma, ideology, guilt, and shame, an explosion can result. The explosion can be minor and leave you slightly frazzled, or it can be massive and leave your bodily ego totally destroyed (i.e. schizophrenic). For more see Michael Sharp, Ego Explosion, 2014, The Blog of Michael Sharp, Available: http://www.michaelsharp.org/ego-explosion/. Also http://www.thespiritwiki.com/Egoic_Explosion and Grof and Grof, Spiritual Emergency: When Personal Transformation Becomes a Crises, Sharp, Ego Explosion.

[203] I would like to define schizophrenia as the pathological collapse of the bodily ego arising when a damaged bodily ego makes an accidental or ill advised (often entheogen-abuse induced) connection with The Fabric. In this situation, a damaged bodily ego that is not capable of containing higher Consciousness fragments dissolves, to be replaced by pathological connection to noetic streams. For more http://www.thespiritwiki.com/Schizophrenia

Let me tell you, it was an emotional, psychological, and behavioral challenge. The challenge began in 2003 with a traumatic, but ultimately emancipating, experience and continued as I struggle to overcome various connection pathologies caused by the damage and indoctrination of childhood. All in all it was a challenging process of inner revelation, self-healing, ideological deprogramming, and slow alignment that was stark, at times dramatic, but ultimately world shaking and emancipatory.

So what did I do to get through it? Better question, how will you get through it when your time comes? I won't go into all the gory details except to say that in order to get to where I am today I had to clear fears, correct erroneous ideas, eliminate disjunctive behaviours, align my thinking and behaviours with the expectations of my own higher consciousness, and keep my damaged ego in check long enough so that it could use insights from The Fabric to fix itself and heal. Not all at once of course, but a little at a time. Baby steps, really. I handled it by practicing every day and gradually letting the power and the glory shine. I kept my ego in check and let the concepts and insights from mystical connection and scholarly analysis gradually transform the fabric of my physical, intellectual, and emotional being. I couldn't just let it come shining through full blast. Like Indiana Jones hopping over a tessellated stone floor to steal the treasures of Asia, I had to move carefully, stepping over (and sometimes triggering) the booby traps of fear, misconception, misdirection, and damaged self-esteem. But move I did, and you will, too. Just practice every day and take baby steps. And be realistic. It takes time and it is complicated to sort out. Not only that, it is a fair amount of work and struggle. Personal healing, disciplined study, healthy family environment, authentic family support,[204] careful observation, past-life

---

[204] I say *authentic family support* here just to highlight the idea that there is a difference between authentic support and inauthentic support. Authentic support is support that lifts you up and makes you feel a) better about yourself and b) more empowered about your place here on Earth. Inauthentic support is typically presented as authentic

preparation, and a host of other factors enter the mix. But baby steps forward will help with everything. Just keep swimming, as Dory from the animated movie *Finding Nemo* says. *As you gradually move forward, the intelligence and insights of higher Consciousness will gradually transform your thinking, your behaviours, and even your environment.* As this transformation occurs, more Light will shine in and it will become easier and easier to understand and move forward. Practice makes perfect and baby steps allow you to process, understand, and ground. Couple practice and baby steps with a little perseverance and patience and you have everything you need to meet the emotional, psychological, and behavioral challenges, even if you come from a not-so-great background.

Communication Challenges

So, effusive flow, unformed lumps, notions that we have to be passive receptacles, ideology, the powerful nature of consciousness, and the intellectual / emotional / psychological challenges that accompany contact all bubbled and boiled in the preternatural mystical stew. All these posed challenges to forward movement and the goal of establishing persistent connection; but of course, these were not the only challenges. An additional challenge was (and is) the problem of communication. I cannot tell a lie, one of the biggest challenges that I have had to overcome is the challenge of communicating what I have learned and the work that I have done. Indeed, I sometimes feel that everything else, from healing the wounds of childhood to taming the spiritual flow, pale in comparison to the challenge of communicating to the world.

The question at this point is, what is so challenging about communicating all this spiritual insight? Isn't it a simple case of open your mouth and speak. Not so! Challenges to

---

support by the toxic people giving it, but it is actually intended to undermine and even destroy. If you want to move forward you need to learn the difference between authentic and inauthentic support.

communication are real and come from three general areas. There is the **intellectual challenge** that arises from the beleaguered/damaged spiritual/intellectual fabric of this planet; there is **political challenge** that arises from the ongoing external resistance one faces to expressing Truth (both from political/economic elites and the general population); finally, there are the **emotional and psychological challenges** that come when trying to ground, process, and express the high spiritual Truths of creation with concept, ideas, and archetypes that simply cannot contain the full light. Let us look at each of these challenges briefly in turn starting with intellectual challenges.

Intellectual Challenges to Communication

As you will recall, in an earlier section we covered the intellectual challenges of sorting it out and grounding it down. That's a big challenge. As for the *intellectual challenges to communication,* these are manifold and complex as well. **First**, consider the damaged spiritual-intellectual fabric of this planet. This is going to sound like a heretical statement to some, but in my view there is no pure spiritual system that exists on this planet. Some are *pure thievery,* designed to bilk shame filled Hollywood A-listers, and anybody else who has the money, of their hard earned cash. Some are authentic, but personal failures of the "messengers," social, political, and professional limitations, lack of technology, or external interference have impeded the flow. Some are ancient and originally true, but have been corrupted and twisted over the years and centuries to support a venal status quo. As a result of all these issues, our extant spiritualities fail to pass muster. Extant spiritualities do not lead to authentic spiritual connection[205] and they do not support perpetual, permanent, realization, identification,

---

[205] And don't tell me they do because if you say they do, I'll want proof. Show me the self-realized members. Show me the awakened Gods. And please, don't elevate your personal favorite talk show celebrity rock star rich person as an example of enlightened connection. These folks may display partial connection at best, or they may be no more self-realized than a rock. Monetary/worldly success does not necessarily equate with spiritual advancement, especially when the success is in unaligned occupations and professions antagonistic to authentic spiritual connection.

union, samadhi with your superior higher Self. Without going into any details, but trying to be as comprehensive as possible, let me just say...

1. Extant spiritual systems are confused, disorienting, filled with misconception, soaked in ideology, and brimming with **cosmic sexism**.[206]

2. Because of this, you can't rely on extant systems to learn about, understand, or communicate about important spiritual topics. The concepts have too much baggage, too much misconception, and if you use them you risk invoking fear, confusion, misconception, sexism, racism, and even homophobia in yourself and others.

So what do you do?

Well, as already noted, you build a new system, not because you want to,[207] and certainly not because it makes you feel special,[208] but because if you want to talk about spiritual things, you have to. There just is no other way. Take the Christian concept of **sin** as an example. Sin is a good concept. In fact, it is an important one. Defined formally I would say that sin is any action that a) is out of alignment with your RMC and b) causes injury or harm to another living being. The idea that you are doing something "wrong" (i.e. something your higher Self doesn't like) to something or someone else is a good idea to have, because it is real. There is such a thing as right and wrong, in relation to Consciousness. The problem is, the word sin has been corrupted. Instead of defining sin in a divinely appropriate

---

[206] Cosmic sexism is a term used to describe the importation and/or presence of sexist categorizations in spiritual discussions. Cosmic sexism appears when human categories of gender are imposed on spiritual ideas inappropriately. See http://www.thespiritwiki.com/Cosmic_Sexism

[207] There are a lot of other fun things I could have been doing besides this, let me tell you.

[208] In fact, exactly the opposite is true. Building it proper leads to recognition of our collective divinity and the simple fact that we are all sparks of divine consciousness. If you build it right, you are automatically led away from bloated egoic self-esteem and faulty identification with bodily ego. If you build it right, you realize we are all bright sparks of powerful divine Consciousness. The only difference is, some of us have been slimed with mud and now our light doesn't shine. To fix that, all you have to do is clear the mud off. You see, you just can't be "special," in the hierarchical sense of that word, on a planet where you are surrounded by fully realized sparks of divine God Consciousness, now can you?

way by saying that sin is something you commit when you don't listen to your own higher Self, sin is redefined as failing to follow the rules or failing to respect authority! This corrupted idea still has the seed of the original idea (i.e. sin is going against something higher than the little you of your physical body) only the purview has been restricted to defying authority. The message is clear: to defy authority is a sin!

Once the concept of sin has been corrupted in this fashion, you cannot use it in a conversation without clarification. Because the word "sin" has come to mean "it is wrong to defy authority," you can't use the concept to understand/communicate unless you a) redefine it or b) come up with a new concept.[209] Either way, that is a lot of work. And the idea of "sin" is just one idea. The spiritual fabric of this planet is so messed up that you need to refresh or redefine hundreds of concepts. You can't use extant systems as they lie and are corrupt, so you got to work up something new or spend time sorting out the old. Whether you adopt what I have painstakingly put together,[210] you come up with your own reconceptualization and understanding, or you choose to stay in your current tradition,[211] you have an intellectual challenge ahead.

To be sure, the damaged spiritual-intellectual fabric of this planet is a problem with regards to talking about spirituality, but it is not the only intellectual challenge to communication. Even if everything was in proper order in your own

---

[209] Most of the time I choose to come up with a new concept. I do that because some concepts are inflated by the ego of the creator, some were not properly defined in the first place, and some remain complex and ill-defined. In most cases it is usually easier to just throw it all on the scrap heap and start with a fresh lump of clay. Sin is different. The old energy concept of sin as defiance of authority is The System's foundational keystone. Yank that keystone out and the whole system starts to crumble.

[210] You can get a summary and overview of the conceptual bricks I provide by perusing the SpiritWiki. See http://www.thespirtwiki.com.

[211] Which you can if you want. I know I say that extant spiritual traditions, especially those with ancient roots, are corrupt, I would also say that there's a lot of awesome Truth there as well if you dig around. The problem is, if you keep your spiritual tradition, you have to dig around. Whether that's more or less work for *you* I cannot say, because it depends on where you are at right now. I'll just say, "it is work either way," and let you decide for yourself.

spiritual/intellectual space, a **second intellectual** challenge to communication is the challenge of syncretism.[212] According to the FreeDictionary.com website, syncretism is "reconciliation or fusion of differing systems of belief, as in philosophy or religion...." Thus, **syncretism** is when you can merge/meld spiritual systems to the point where people embedded in one system can speak clearly with people embedded in other systems. Obviously, if we want to contribute to global transformation and human unity, as I do, a global discussion on spirituality is necessary, but currently impossible. Jews, Christians, Muslims, Buddhists, and so on, don't talk to each other, not because they necessarily don't want to, but because we don't all speak the same spiritual language. If we do want to talk about spirituality we have to use the concepts provided in our local language and local spirituality. This makes it almost impossible to talk to someone from another cultural/ethnic space, and obviously makes communication with the world a major challenge. How can you transform and unite humanity when you can't have a common discussion? The answer is, you can't. You might hope and pray, and you may even have the certainty that comes with divine revelation, but if there is no syncretism, you're stuck. As long as there are major language barriers and multiple spiritual systems, global transformation and unity are impossible.[213]

So what do you do? As already noted, you build a new system. You come up with new concepts and ideas not because you want to, and certainly not because it makes you feel special, but because if you want to talk about spiritual things to anybody other than members of your own family and church, you have

---

[212] Syncretism is achieved by a) creating a common global language that people from all cultures can speak and then b) creating new, neutral, and simple (so they can easily be translated) bricks (concepts) referring to key spiritual ideas. Once you've done that, and assuming good penetration of the English language, and some strong technical supports, then —boom—, instant global communication. Simple.

[213] Of course, major progress has been made. Now the technological and linguistic infrastructures are in place; technologically we have social media which provides the potential for wide scale and rapid global communication. Linguistically, I think I can safely assume all communities have enough people who speak English and their native tongue to be able to translate rapidly. The only thing left is the conceptual bricks and mortar.

to. You need to find new concepts and new ideas and you need to find ways to speak that communicate and connect. And that's a challenge, but it is a challenge that I have been working on right from the start, and it is a challenge that I believe can be overcome.

Take the LP idea of "connection" as an example. Connection is a simple word in the English language, and a very fundamental Truth/Reality of our manifest existence. The idea of connection is simple. Thus one does not have to be a native speaker of the language to understand. Even those just learning a language would know what it meant in their own spiritual system. Once it is established that the word connection refers to the connection between bodily ego and spiritual ego, then it can easily be translated into one's native tongue. Once there is a general global understanding of the word *connection*, syncretism is achieved. It is work getting there to be sure, but it is possible, in this lifetime, if we all get to work and do what we came here to do.

Connection takes the idea of mystical union with God, Consciousness, Krishna, or whatever you want to call it, and reduces it to a simple brick, connection. This simple, basic, brick can then be used to begin a discussion with others, either with or without translation. If there are enough English speakers around you, you can just use the concept raw. If not, you can easily translate. Either way, the LP concept of connection, and other concepts developed over the years, help with syncretism and communication. It makes a spiritual discussion easy, allows you to link concepts from multiple spiritual traditions,[214] and when you consider the massive

---

[214] An excellent example of this is a response from a physician in India Dr. Ranjan Solanki of the Mahatma Ghandi Institute of Medical Sciences, to a paper I wrote detailing some of the basic LP concepts. This shows the power of syncretic communication to unify, educate, and even transform. I include his response email below.

Thank you so much for sharing this wonderful article. The CQ concept was enthralling....! I am running a mind body medicine Clinic in Sewagram, Wardha, India. Your article will help me explain certain queries by my patients...! Individual connection experience will lead to global transformation.....very true! The root cause behind all physical and mental disorders can be traced to the level of disconnected ness one is

potential of current social media technologies, makes that discussion potentially explosive.

Political and Social Challenges

Besides intellectual challenges to communication, there are also political challenges. As already noted, authentic spirituality is threatening to the status quo[215] because authentic spirituality <u>connects</u>. Authentic spirituality brings the people more into alignment with Consciousness. When alignment and connection occurs, emancipation results. When emancipation results, one is freed from illusion and self-delusion. And, when one is freed from illusion and self-delusion, transformation results. When one becomes connected and aligned, everything that is not right about the world comes into clear focus. When one becomes connected, one is driven to change, and the change that one is driven towards is not compatible with elite interests. Alignment means you can't exploit child labour. Alignment means you cannot lie and dissemble. Alignment means you cannot enrich yourself while the rest of the globe suffers. Connection means you are present and empowered to change all this. The elites know this. This is why, as we have seen in the case of Jesus, they put such great effort into controlling and containing The Word. Elite effort to control and contain means resistance. To be frank, expressing and discussing authentic spirituality makes one a target. The truth is you can talk about spirituality all you want, as long as you are impotent and ineffective. *As soon as you start leading yourself and others towards authentic connection, heresy is the charge and resistance is the result.* In the past, the connected might have been burned alive. Nowadays, and unless you live in one of the backward hellholes, social ridicule and professional censure are usually the only result. Still, even if the "milder"

---

experiencing...... very true! **Dr. Ranjan Choudhary**

[215] Sosteric, <u>Dangerous Memories: Slavery, Mysticism, and Transformation</u>. See also Sosteric, The Sociology of Mysticism.

and more modern forms of punishment and control are the only things you face, it's still painful, and it can still destroy you. So, it is important to be aware.

But anyway...

I don't want to get into long winded detail about the political challenges one faces in constructing and communicating an authentic spirituality, I just want to point out that as we move forward we all face political challenges. If you talk openly about this stuff, you experience resistance. That's changing of course, and quite rapidly now. More and more people are finding their spouses, adult children, and friends open to new ideas and new concepts. More and more people, even the shackled top members of the high elite poohbahs, are realizing the deceptions and waking themselves up; but, it is not over yet, and you may as yet experience resistance. If so, recognize it for what it is, remove yourself from any physical, emotional, or psychological threat that you may feel, and don't push. Protect yourself, find another space to inhabit, and chill. When it is their time, people will wake up. If you push, you're just wasting your energy and possibly opening yourself up to violence. Right now, just protect yourself. You will know when it is time to start talking because you will find a more fertile field.

Emotional/Psychological Challenges

By now you will realize that there are a lot of challenges to face. From challenges involved in connecting and handling the flow all the way through to political and social resistance, walking and talking about an authentic path is not a straightforward or easy process, at least not yet anyway. Things are changing and it is getting easier, but it is going to be a challenge for a few years yet. Moving forward you are still going to want to be mindful; there are many challenges and obstacles and if you want to meet the challenges and overcome the obstacles, you want to be mindful and aware; and, if you need it, you want to get the support.

Before closing I just want to mention that in addition to all the challenges we have covered so far, there are two final challenges that you have to be aware of, and these are the emotional and psychological challenges of communication. I have already mentioned the emotional and psychological challenges of understanding. As I noted above, the toxicity that I experienced damaged my ego, lowered my self-esteem, and instilled religious fears/misconceptions that initially prevented me from connecting and consequently threatened to corrupt the information. The emotional and psychological challenges to communicating come from the same cuts and revolve around damaged self-esteem, self-doubt, and lack of confidence. Looking at the corpus now you might wonder that I ever had an issue communicating, but I did. Right from the start I was worried and uncertain. Could I do this? Was what I was saying truthful? Was I getting it right? Who was I to be writing such things?

I know many people have these intellectual and emotional challenges. I know that these challenges come from the same toxic place; a substandard childhood; parents who undermine instead of nurture; a school system intent on breaking the children down. I also know that many people find these intellectual and emotional challenges and blockages very difficult to overcome. To be sure, I had these challenges as well. I lacked confidence, questioned my character, and was riddled with self-doubt for a good part of my life. I won't kid you, it took many years to overcome the blockages. Indeed, it has only been very recently where I have come to be able to express and communicate with full realization. And even now, only under certain conditions. I have no doubt it is/will be the same for you. If there is one thing that is attacked ferociously on this planet, it is our ability to communicate. Things are changing, and fast now, but we've all still got challenges. From the housewife who struggles to express to Mr. Big S. in Hollywood, we're struggling to get it all out. And that's OK. It will all work out in right time. For now, just believe in yourself. As long as you don't give up you'll eventually sort it all out and when you do, don't hold back. Deep inside you is a glorious spark of Consciousness. The only thing that spark wants to do is sing, paint, laugh, dance, work, jump, transform, give, and live. The spark is brilliant, bright, and powerful and there's nothing to be afraid of at all. So take a deep breath, set your intent, and fly.

Conclusions

This chapter has been about challenges. As you can see, we all face many challenges walking an authentic path towards authentic connection. If we want to move forward, we have to meet these challenges. There is no other way.

I know it can all seem overwhelming, and while I don't want to minimize the challenges, I do want to say, <u>triumph is within reach</u>. Now more than ever we have what we need to wake up, move forward, and create the world we want to create. We have the technology (computers, internet), we have the economic capability, we have the human power, and we have the divine Consciousness standing by and ready to work. All we have to do is agree on the direction and the divine will unfold. Of course, we still have to work. The divine sees through our eyes, hears through our ears, and works through our hands! If we (and by "we" I mean the human race) don't see, hear, talk, walk, and transform, nothing happens. It is as simple as that.

In closing up this chapter I just want to say three things. I want to express a caution, make a point, and issue a challenge. As for the **cautionary expression**, obviously, if you are a student looking to make a connection with The Fabric of Consciousness, you want to pay attention. There are lots of things you have to pay attention to, lots of things you have to learn, lots of things you have to avoid, and lots of things you have to do. My best advice to you is devote as much of your life to spiritual awakening and activation as you can. And I don't mean just be a student, I mean be a teacher, an artist, a professional, a businessperson, a politician, a lawyer, a mother, a father, devoted to the cause. Read, re-read, meditate, cogitate, rehearse, learn, heal, enlighten, activate, grow, heal, teach, uplift. Use the LP materials if you want or find other worthy materials. Of course I understand you have multiple priorities: work, family, friends, and etc. However, if you want my advice, whatever your priorities are, put spirituality at the front of your daily cue.[216] If you don't, you won't go anywhere. Once you're moving it gets easier, but at the start, there are many challenges. To overcome the challenges you have to put the time in.

As for the point I want to make, it is simply this. When it comes to mystical experience, there is a lot more going on beneath the proverbial surface than we might at first think. If your image of "higher" realities is Church God, if you think human spirituality is about kneeling in pews, going to church socials, prostrating before a guru, or rubbing a Tibetan bowl, you're misinformed. Authentic spirituality is a lot more than that. It is a lot more than employees of the Church say; it is a lot more than Double-N mystics realize; it is a lot more than some people want you to know. I kid you not when I say, moving forward, understanding, communicating, and finally realizing and becoming a fully connected human is a major individual, social, political, and economic challenge. It is a global challenge. If we are to make progress here we need to take a more critical *and* a more open minded approach to things, and we need to work together. More to the point perhaps, if we want to advance our understanding of mystical phenomenon, indeed if we want to become students of spirituality with a view toward authentic spiritual experience, we need to engage with spirituality, religion, and mysticism in the same way we engage with anything else, which is to say scientifically, empirically, and sensibly.

Finally, **I wish to issue a challenge** and the challenge is this,

---

[216] Make sure you always tend to other important priorities, like your child, your spouse, and your job. Find time for devotion, but don't be neglectful of your life, or of others.

transform the world through mystical connection. The world is in crisis and there are good reasons to suggest that authentic mystical experience may be the key to our collective salvation, or at least the fertile ground of our morality and humanity.[217] Certainly it is something worth looking at. As scientists, we have had no problem developing atomic weapons and Orwellian surveillance technologies, but we have demonstrated a cowardly and dismissive lack of concern and appreciation for an area of human experience that is as old as humanity itself. Science as powerful and cowardly avoidance of spirituality and religion is unacceptable. I have said it before and I will say it again; we need to overcome the challenges and break through the barriers so we can all do the work that we came here to do.

---

[217] Sosteric, Dangerous Memories: Slavery, Mysticism, and Transformation. See also Sosteric, The Sociology of Mysticism.

LP Exploration and Exposition Principles

As noted in the last two chapters, dealing with the mystical gusher that was initiated following my initial spiritual clearings was a problem. From the quantity of the information to the power of the Light to the **ideological bleed**[218] through the intellectual, emotional, and political struggles, it was a challenge through and through. I suppose the biggest problem at outset was that I did not fully understand what was going on. It is much easier to talk about the whole process with a degree of lucidity now, but in the early days it was like standing in a hurricane of mystical spew. I did not understand where the information was coming from, I did not understand why it was flowing in such copious quantities, I did not understand the sometimes peculiar quality of the information, and I had no idea what I should do with it all.

Recognizing that there were some problems and challenges, but not fully understanding the nature of these problems at the outset, I decided early on to develop a set of principles and standards upon which to base all Lightning Path writing and spirituality. The idea from the start was to set some standards that not only would guide my work, but that others could use to evaluate my work, the work of others as well, or even their own spiritual work as well. The guidelines are general purpose and primarily aimed at providing a critical foundation for inquiry and practice. The goals was (and is) not only to make sure I am creating something of global value, but also to help others understand, evaluate, and even create high quality and authentic spiritual resources.

I should note at the outset that the principles and standards that

---

[218] Ideological bleed occurs when mystical revelation is corrupted by ideology. This corruption occurs when spiritual truths revealed in the process of inner revelation become tainted with the venal excuses and justifications of the political/economic system. http://www.thespiritwiki.com/Ideological_Bleed

I lay out here did not emerge full blown and all at once but were developed over the course of several years; nor, I should say, is it possible to discuss them all here. Some of the principles and standards I put in *Rocket Scientists' Guide to Authentic Spirituality,* a book that provides a definition of authentic spirituality and a foundation for a productive and grounded spirituality. Some I put in *The Great Awakening: Concepts and Techniques for Successful Spiritual Practice,* a book that provides practical basic technique and concepts that get you properly oriented toward authentic mystical connection and authentic spirituality. Still others I discuss in *Rocket Scientists' Guide to Spiritual Discernment.* Here I can only discuss a limited subset.

With the limited nature of this introductory discussion in mind, here I will discuss what I call **exploration and exposition** (E&E) principles. E&E principles are basically the principles that I used to guide not only my exploration of The Fabric, but also how I would think about, conceptualize, and finally write about it.[219] It might sound strange, but even early in the process I knew there would be traps, pitfalls, and swindles along the road to Shambhala and I knew I had to protect "the work" against nefarious outcomes. I wasn't sure what they all might be, but I knew they would be there and I knew, before I got too far "into it," that I had to do something to protect.

Finally, I will note (and this will be interesting for only some), these principles were not based on any sort of mystical rocket science, deep mystical revelation, or divine spiritual connection. These principles emerged directly out of my training as a sociologist. As a sociologist, you see, I am aware of ideology and social class (group) manipulation. With the clarity of a 4K TV, I see classicism, racism, sexism, genderism, and whatever "ism" you care to invoke, wherever it is. I see it embedded in our political, social, personal, professional, and

---

[219] For more see http://www.thespiritwiki.com/Exploration_and_Exposition_Principles

entertainment worlds. I see it in Hollywood, in literature, and in education. I'm sure most of my sociological colleagues would agree with the statement, we see it everywhere, especially in religion! We've seen it since Karl Marx declared religion to be an opiate. So as soon as I started to make a connection, as soon as I took a critical look at the flow, I knew something was wrong. What I saw set my sociological senses tingling, as my sociological training kicked in, I began to formulate my E&E principles. What follows is a record of how my sociological (and to a lesser extent, Humanistic Psychology) impacted my exploration and analysis. I believe these principles are solid and present in the Lightning Path corpus at all levels. It is up to the reader and student to judge for themselves.

No Rocket Science

The first principle that I set down when my sociological senses started tingling was that the Lightning Path should contain no rocket science. By that I mean to say that official Lightning Path resources would have no complicated gobbledygook, no technical jargon, no intricate grammatical turns of phrase, and no unnecessary linguistic or metaphoric puffery. In other words, and because I view all forms of EPMO saturated discourse as obfuscatory, Lightning Path materials were to be accessible and fully exposed.

The full exposure of the LP is accomplished in two ways. On the one hand the LP uses grounded and simple prose to teach and convey information. On the other hand, all LP concepts are fully exposed on the SpiritWiki. That is, all LP concepts and ideas are defined on an open web Wiki. Because all LP concepts and ideas are defined out in the open where everybody can access, there is nothing esoteric or obscured. There are no intervening waypoints; there is no need to decipher and decode. The entire world can see for itself exactly what it is I am talking about at any time they wish (assuming, for now, that they can read English).

The reason for this principle is simple enough to see, at least for a sociologist. Hiding ideas, whether you hide them by enclosing them in a lodge, obscuring them with fancy words, or simply locking them away in monasteries or behind price walls, makes ideology and manipulation easier. Opaque teachings make it easier to create, disseminate, and preserve ideology. Just briefly, when spiritual materials are labeled "esoteric," when they are complicated, obtuse, difficult to read, hard to understand, obscured by conceptual puffery, and time consuming to process, they confuse readers, limit accessibility, and wall off the truth so only the "privileged few" can access, and only the even more privileged few can modify, manipulate, and control without outside scrutiny. People lead busy lives and complicated, esoteric, garbled, and confusing mystical texts confuse, intimidate, and turn people away. Self-esteem may also take a hit as they ask themselves "Why can't I understand this?" They may blame themselves for deficiencies actually present in the materials themselves. Who wants to struggle with stuff that makes you feel stupid, after all?

Of course, not everybody is turned away; but, even if you choose to try to sort out muddy teachings, other problems manifest. EPMO, for example, clouds the issues, murkies the water, and makes it hard to understand. More to the point, EPMO makes it harder to test and evaluate. Instead of being offered clear and easy to understand concepts so that you can immediately evaluate and assess (against, for example, your own personal experience), you waste time and energy trying to figure it out. If you don't figure it out on your own, you'll either construct an elaborate self-delusion to assuage/submerge the feelings of failure, you'll blame yourself for deficiencies actually present in the materials and/or the presentation, or you cave in and listen to somebody else's "expert/hierophant" opinion to tell you what it all means. The point is, Rocket Science (or EPMO, as you prefer) limits understanding, perpetuates confusion, makes it hard to figure things out without the assistance of "hierophants" from above (in the social/political hierarchy), and makes judging the quality of the materials very difficult. It's a waste of time, energy, and effort.

Fortunately, it is not this way on the Lightning Path. As you will discover as you wind your way through LP materials, even the most complicated and esoteric spiritual, cosmological, economic, and scientific concepts are explained in an accessible, grounded, and open fashion so that everyone can understand. This eliminates all the problems associated with EPMO and thoroughly democratizes mysticism. It makes the pursuit of spiritual experience and enlightenment easy for you (for anybody), speeds up your progress, and gives you a healthy shot of self-esteem in the process. Instead of wasting time and effort trying to extricate yourself from esoteric circles, or worrying if the problem is you, you can focus on the concepts and practices in the materials themselves. This is a powerful thing. It means you'll make much faster forward progress than you otherwise might if you had to deal with biased and exclusionary EPMO.

No Hierarchy and No Privilege

The second E&E principle that guides LP writing and exploration is *no hierarchy and no privilege*. That is, you will not find anything anywhere in any official LP resource that supports, justifies, or otherwise helps create structures of hierarchy and privilege. There is no nonsense about "being chosen," no intimations that "only the strong survive," no suggestion that some are more worthy than others, no patriarchy or silly ideas that men are better than women (or vice versa), no implicit (or explicit) racism, no justifications of judgment and punishment, and no attempt to convince you that some people are "smarter than," "better than," "stronger than," or otherwise "more than" anybody else. More to the point, there is no suggestion anywhere in any Lightning Path resource that some people deserve to be highly rewarded because of their "superiority", while others deserve poverty and suffering for their stupid inferior weaknesses. The spiritual message of the LP is un-muddied by corrupt and opportunistic justification, venal socio-economic interests, and/or unresolved emotional or psychological pathology. Accept it or not, the message of the Lightning Path is crystal clear, precise, and goes something like this.

We all issue from the same source.

We are all members of the same family of Spirit.

We are all expressions of divine light.

We are all equal in consciousness.

We all deserve a life free of violence, abuse, and disregard.

We all deserve a life full of health, happiness, prosperity, education, and wealth.

In other words, we are all fundamentally glorious, equal, and worthy in the eyes of God, Consciousness, and creation. Take it or leave it, like it or not, *we are all individualized monads in a cosmic spiritual collective.*

It should be emphasized here that this fundamental collective equality of monadic consciousness and my concomitant refusal to prop up the status quo does not arise out of personally selected political, economic, or social morality. Rather, it emerges as a logical consequence of the *nature* of who we are as sparks of awareness within a divine Fabric of Consciousness. The Truth, just like every mystic before me has said, is that we are all sparks of creator consciousness. I outline the truth of our nature and identity in detail in the four volumes of *The Book of Light*,[220] but I can summarize it here by saying the truth is simply this.

- We are all sparks of creator consciousness existing as, and emerging out of the same glorious Fabric of Consciousness.

---

[220] Sharp, The Book of Light: The Nature of God, the Structure of Consciousness, and the Universe within You., *The Book of Light: The Nature of God, the Structure of Consciousness, and the Universe Within You.*

- We are all instantiated points of light emerging out of the same "level" and point of existence.

- We are all identical in our spiritual brightness.

- We are all strong, powerful, and competent in the glory and power of our full light.

True, we all express differently. We all follow different paths, we all develop different skills, and we end up as different entities; but nothing, and when I say nothing, I mean nothing ever changes the fact that *we are one* in the glorious Fabric of Consciousness, *we are equal* in the bright expression of that consciousness, *we are worthy* of nothing but the best of everything, and *we are strong* in the power and glory of our light.

You may want to pause for a moment or two and repeat this basic truth just so you remember it and are clear about it.

We are one.

We are worthy.

We are equal.

We are strong.

Remember. Nothing you do or say can change who you are. Also remember, basing the Lightning Path teachings on this basic spiritual truth, in fact, basing your life on this basic spiritual truth, is an essential step toward Samadhi, or realizing and identifying with the reality of who we really are. And of course, once we finally realize that, the old world comes to end. But, I'm jumping ahead. Before we get to that, a couple more E&E principles.

No Gender / No Ethnicity

As noted above, initial challenges with the mystical process led me to formulate certain *exploration and exposition* principles that I used to guide the initial development of the LP. No rocket science and no hierarchy and privilege are the first two principles. The third principle used to inform the development of the Lightning Path is this: no sexism, no gender, and no race/ethnicity. On the Lightning Path, you won't find any suggestion that gender or race/ethnicity is important to spirituality at all. In other words, there are no sexist spiritual ideas or archetypes. To be as blunt as possible, God isn't male and Gaia isn't female, nor does your skin color make a sniff of difference to the bright light of your soul. The reason for this is simply because when it comes to spirituality, gender and ethnicity are irrelevant. The truth is, you are an incarnated spark of <u>light</u> seated in a powerful physical vehicle. The light, the Consciousness that animates your body, has no gender, sex, or ethnicity at all! It is just light, awareness, power, and compassion. The body that you are seated in has gender, that's true, but

a) your body is just a vehicle

b) skin color is nothing more than an indication of the amount of sun your ancestors got

c) sex is only a part of reality at this low physical level of physical creation and

d) sex and gender are choices that you make (usually before you incarnate) based on past experience and personal preference.[221]

---

[221] Yes, I am saying that you choose to be gay. Don't freak out. I understand that sleeping people use the idea of "choice" as a foundation for repressive attempts to "cure," but that's messed up. True, you are born gay, but you also chose to incarnate in that energy usually long before you were born. So what? It is the kind of choice you make when you choose your car. You can drive a pink car, or a blue car, or a purple car, or a black car, or whatever. It is just a car, it is just a choice, and it is just sex. Condemning somebody for their sexual orientation and / or trying to cure them of their choice makes about as much sense as condemning somebody because they drive a red Volkswagen, or forcing them to choose another vehicle even when they love the one they are in. It just makes no sense at all.

And, just in case you are having some trouble with what I'm saying here, let me rephrase it.

There's nothing wrong with being gay. Being gay doesn't change your light, your love, your connection, or your power. Being gay just puts you in a different vehicle, that's all. Whether you are gay, straight, or somewhere in between, if you want my advice, quit wasting energy on this issue, accept and rejoice in diversity, get over it, and get on with the show.

Above and beyond the physical world, sex and ethnicity are insignificant and unimportant. The truth is, Consciousness is just light and your body is just a vehicle. You need to get this through your head. You need to separate your monadic consciousness (your so called "higher" self) from your consciousness as embodied in the vehicle (your bodily consciousness) and you need to understand that you incarnate in your physical unit so you can have fun and create in the physical world, period. How you choose to manifest that creative effort, whether it is through a female body, a male body, a transsexual body, or whatever, is merely a choice that has no spiritual consequence or cosmic significance at all. It is, you must know, exactly the same as choosing a car. Some people like white cars, some people like red cars, some people like pink Cadillacs, some people like Ford Mustangs, and that's all there is to it. Of course, there are reasons why we choose one car or another. Perhaps we want a fast ride. Perhaps we are looking for something easy on gas. Whatever it is, ultimately it doesn't really matter what car you choose to drive. It is a choice and nothing more.

It is the same with your physical unit. What you have between your legs and who you decide to share it with is irrelevant when it comes to God, consciousness, creation, and the work that you came here to do. Of course, this doesn't mean there isn't a difference between the sexes, or that culture doesn't play a role in human experience. There are a few differences between the male and female bodies; Indian culture, for example, is different than European culture; and these differences are significant, to a point. This also doesn't mean that you can't make gender and cultural differences bigger if you want. Little boy and girl babies are more similar than they are different, at least in the beginning! When they are born, they have exactly the same emotions, intellect, and needs and they respond exactly the same to everything (i.e. they scream and cry when they don't get their needs met). However, give the boy a blue blanket and the girl a pink, tell the boy to be strong and manly and the girl to be soft and feminine, encourage the boy to jump around and rough house and keep the girl close and cuddled, and you will *create* a difference, maybe even a big difference between the sexes that didn't exist at the start.

In sociology, this is the difference between *sex* and *gender*. Sex is what we are born with: gender is what **Agents of Socialization**[222] make of it. Sex is the instrument between your legs; gender is the massive social reality that we build around that instrument. Sex is a little difference; gender, at least as constructed on this Earth, is a vast divide.

And is that wrong? Is creating a (massive) gender difference a problem? Not necessarily. If you create that difference and then tell women that the only thing they are good for is spreading their legs, cooking your supper, washing your clothes, and making your babies, then yes that's a bad thing. If you create a difference and then tell men they shouldn't feel, shouldn't care, shouldn't be parents, and should just work hard until they drop dead of a heart attack, then yes it is bad. But, if you create difference and then celebrate that difference...

If you create difference in order to bask in the glory of the male and female form...

If you create difference in order to enhance our creative work...

If you create difference to make sex fun, exciting, and hot...

If you create difference for cultural variety...

Then how is that a problem?

We are creative beings and we make things all the time. Whether we make a building, a body, or a society, it really all comes down to why we do it and what we do with it when we're done. If we make gender different in order to feed The System, then yes, that's a problem. However, if we make gender difference so we can enjoy ourselves and celebrate our

---

[222] An Agent of Socialization is an individual or institution tasked with the replication of the social order. See http://www.thespiritwiki.com/Agents_of_Socialization

differences, then no, it's not a big deal. We can make what we want, for reasons that we want, whenever we want, just so long as we (a) do it for reasons aligned with Consciousness and (b) end up with something that enhances creation and reduces suffering. It is also this way with gender. If you create separation between the sexes so you can exploit people, and if you end up with a repressed, suppressed, and depressed physical unit as a result, then bad on you. However, if you create separation between the sexes so you can enhance our collective experience and if you end up with a joyous creative dance of creation, then good. *Be what you want to be, create what you want to create, just do it for the right reasons so you can exist in an aligned relationship with Consciousness.*

And that's really all I have to say about gender and race/ethnicity. I would like to end this brief overview of the spiritual non-significance of gender and race by saying two things. One, in addition to putting sex, gender, and race in proper spiritual perspective, the LP also has a political position when it comes to gender and ethnicity and that position is total equality. As per the description of The Fabric of Consciousness provided in my *Book of Light*, and according to the second E&E principle of no hierarchy and no privilege, the LP is free of any form of gender-race justified exclusion, hierarchy, or privilege. On the Lightning Path there is no suggestion that men are better than women, women are better than men, or white is better than black. On the Lightning Path, men do not hide in secret clubhouses and women do not huddle in exclusionary social cliques. On the Lightning Path, men and women of all ethnic groupings and social classes work together to uplift and transform the planet. Thus, rather than dividing men and women in an attempt to control, dominate, exclude, and exploit, similarities are honored, created differences are celebrated when appropriate, and the sexes are brought together to uplift and transform. You will find this is true from the most superficial LP guidance on emotions and chakras to the deepest cosmological truths of God and creation. On the

LP, we put sex and gender in its proper place, removing the cancerous element and celebrating the creative glory that exists behind the exploitative manipulation that has characterized sex and gender on this Earth for so many thousands of years.

The second and final thing I want to emphasize here is that everything I've said about sex and gender also applies to skin color and ethnicity. On the LP, we don't play into ethnicity at all, for any reason. Like your choice of sexual expression, your choice of skin color and ethnicity is nothing more than a choice of vehicle. Being born in this country or that country, being born with this skin color or the other really, from a spiritual perspective, is no big deal. It is what you choose to do with the difference that counts. Just as with gender, you can make a big difference or a little difference of it. Whether that is right or wrong, aligned or not, really depends on why you do it and what you end up with. If you choose to make a big deal of ethnic difference in order to justify enslaving a population and exploiting their work power, then that's a bad thing. However, if you choose to make a big deal of ethnic difference so you can experience different cultures, different foods, and different expressions, without demeaning or exploiting others, then that is a good thing. Difference (or lack of it) is not the spiritual problem. What you do with that difference is.[223]

No Compromise and No Strings

So far we have covered three E&E principles that have guided the development of the LP, these being no rocket science, no hierarchy and privilege, and no gender/ethnicity. The fourth and final E&E principle upon which the LP is based is this: *the*

---

[223] I don't want anybody taking what I've just said here and suggesting that, because we choose gender and ethnicity, we also choose suffering, violence, and/or poverty as some sort of life lesson. We don't. Suffering, violence, and poverty are caused by the actions of people on this planet and are an unfortunate reality that we, if we want to be on this planet, have to suffer through because there aren't currently any better options. It shouldn't be like that, however. Since we are all connected, since we are all love and compassion, and since we are all power, we shouldn't take actions that hurt other people and we shouldn't create conditions that cause suffering, violence, and poverty. We are responsible and we have to change that. We have to create better options for everybody and we have to do it now.

truth and nothing but the truth, no compromise, and no strings attached. The first part of this two-part principle (i.e. the truth, no compromise) means that on the one hand LP resources are written to express the highest truths possible at all times. That is, every effort is made to be one hundred percent spiritually and scientifically accurate in everything that is said. This is not so much of an issue when dealing with science. Scientists must live within the basic expectation that they tell the truth. They don't always succeed because sometimes bias and error creep in,[224] but expression of the truth is a basic principle and they do strive to fulfill it. However, while science has committed to truth, when it comes to human spirituality, epistemological standards fall through the floor. When it comes to human spirituality, it is very much the case that anything goes. That is, in the realm of religion, spirituality, and mysticism, you can say just about anything you want and get away with it. All sorts of nonsense from "God is a patriarchal bully who will burn you in hell for an eternity if you do not do what you are told" to "you'll be reborn as a slug if you're not a good girl" seems to be accepted without much question. The standards for rational and reasonable truth in the area of spirituality, religion, and mysticism are low indeed.

Now, there are a number of reasons for this, not the least of which is that both mystics and scholars "cop out" when it comes to trying to express and understand the truths. There is, curiously, the often stated assumption that the mystical apprehension of God, consciousness, and creation simply cannot be understood from a rational and scientific perspective. Mysticism, spirituality, God, and consciousness are, as so many researchers in this area have said, ineffable or "beyond words."

---

[224] For one example of a rather significant error, see for Mike Sosteric, "Ding Dong the Alpha Male Is Dead," The Socjourn (2012)., *Ding Dong the Alpha Male is Dead,* an article that discusses how the originator of the term "*alpha male*" has now retracted the term and apologized for his error. Or consider Mike Sosteric, "Gendered Activities, Gender Difference, Gender Exclusion," The Socjourn (2012). This article highlights the prevalent, persistent, and systemic gender bias in psychology and science. For an excellent early discussion of the issue of norms and ideology in science, see Michael J. Mulkay, "Norms and Ideology in Science," Social Science Information 15.4-5 (1976).

As a result, you just cannot pin it down. Therefore, you just have to accept the fact that whatever anybody says about spirituality, God, and consciousness is as valid as what anybody else has to say. One person says it's an abusive God, the other says it's a cold hard universe, and I say it's a loving expression of awareness, compassion, and power, and we're all right, right?

Nonsense!!! Somebody has to be wrong and if you are serious about spiritual progress, you have to face the fact and figure it out. Of course, facing the fact and figuring it out are not necessarily easy things to do. Personally, I think the religion, spirituality, and mysticism of this planet is a huge and ideologically convoluted mess; but just because it's a mess doesn't mean it is impossible to sort it out. As we have seen throughout this book, there are challenges involved, but to jump from the reality of challenge to the defeatist "anything goes" mentality is wrong and irresponsible. This is an unacceptable position that sets the mystic, the scholar, and the general population up for failure and confusion. It is also a rather odd position to take, especially if you are a scientist. If scholars had given up on astronomy, physics, or chemistry saying we're just too stupid to understand the world, where would we be now? We certainly wouldn't live in this technological marvel of a world that we live in now. The point here however isn't to wag fingers; the point is simply to state that the LP does not cop out when it comes to exposition of mystical truth, nor does it water down its strong claims to represent the truth. The explicit and ostensible goal of the LP is nothing less than the complete and grounded (dare I say scientific) explication of mystical/spiritual truth. On the issue of discovering and understanding truth, there can be no compromise.

Of course, saying that truth is the goal and actually attaining the goal are two different things. Like science's normative goal to tell the truth of things, the LP goal to tell the truth of things is more of a desiderata, statement of process, and affirmation of commitment than it is a reference to an actual, attainable, destination. We are after the truth that is for sure. But do we ever reach the "truth station?" The answer is an unequivocal no. Just like science is an eternal process of discovery and revelation, so is spirituality a process of eternal discovery and revelation. We exist and manifest in vast cosmos of powerful, manifested, Consciousness. There is simply no way that any single part of that Fabric, that any single monad, can ever map it all out. It's impossible. The Fabric, which is "I," exists as an object of identity *and* exploration. Even when we ascend, even when we connect and realize, the exploration doesn't end. It just changes. But just because we're explorers, just because it never ends, doesn't mean we don't try or that we don't make progress. Just like historians explore the past or psychologists explore the mind,[225] mystics explore Consciousness. And just like no historian or psychologist can "see and say it all," so it is with the spirituality, mysticism, and the LP. It is simply a question of what you focus on and how much detail you provide. Just so you know, as far as the LP goes, the focus is Connection; in this regard, there is as much sociological, psychological, historical, and physical detail as we need to make sure we facilitate connection.

The second part of this fourth and last E&E principle (i.e. the truth and nothing but, no compromise and no strings attached) means simply that the Lightning Path does not put hooks into you. It is a common phenomenon among spiritual teachers and religious paths to put emotional and psychological hooks out. In order to get your loyalty, and your dollars, they will stroke your ego, tell you that you are special, tell you that they are the only ones that have the truth, tell you that you are chosen, offer you power, money, sex, and so on. In general, they will tell you just what they think they need to tell you to get you to send your energy and money their way. It is a simple case of emotional and psychological manipulation, and all old energy institutions,

---

[225] Or, as is more likely these days, how to control people.

from cults to established spiritual and even business institutions (e.g. Hollywood) do it. If you have self-esteem issues, and in this world, who doesn't, you will be easily hooked. Call it whatever you want, but it is emotional manipulation pure and simple.

Fortunately, the LP is not like that. On the Lightning Path we refuse to put out hooks and attach strings. Although you will get the message that you are powerful, brilliant, sparks of divine consciousness, we will not tell you that you are special in that regard in any way. Indeed, let me make this crystal clear for you so there is absolutely no possibility of misinterpretation. You are not chosen for any reason; you are not more special in any way; you have no special invitation to an end-of-the world party; God doesn't love you more than he loves all his other children; spirit doesn't play favourites.

The truth is, you are no different than anyone else.

The truth is, we are all "old souls."

The truth is, we have all incarnated a thousand times before.

The truth is, we each have eons of creative experience.

The truth is, we are powerful sparks of creator consciousness, and we all have amazing things to offer this world.

The truth is, we are all equal members of the same glorious family of spirit and we don't have to prove anything to anybody in order to claim our birthright. The only thing we have to do is *realize* the truth of our collective divinity and unfold and express it in this world. No matter what anybody else has ever told you, that is all there is to it. Basically, we have to get the God that is inside us all, out. The LP can help with that, or not. It is your choice whether you want to continue on from here at all, and if you do whether you want this path or some other path. Whatever you choose, it is your choice. Feel free to make a right choice, a wrong choice, a choice now, a choice later, or whatever. Remember, no hooks. However, I will tell you this: You are not going to be punished for making a wrong choice and you are not going to be elevated above the crowd for making a right choice. If you make a right choice you are going to get closer to your divinity; if you make a wrong choice you are going to get farther away from said divinity. That is all. Make the choice that takes you home, or not. And if you make a mistake, realize it, and make a different choice next time. That's all there is to it. Relax, take a deep breath, calm down, and feel free to make your choice unencumbered by ideological manipulation, emotional baggage, or fears that your choice is final in any way. It's just a choice. If you find you've made the wrong one, or if down the road you want to change your path, pause and make a different choice.

That's all there is to it.

Stay.

Go.

Come back.

Leave again.

Find your own way.

Do whatever!

You are a being of powerful awareness, compassion, power, and bliss. No matter what you choose, nothing is going to change your position in creation, and nothing is going to harm your immortal soul. Of course your body, that's a different matter. In the physical world choices and actions have (sometimes irreversible) consequences. So think about where you want to go; think about the consequences of your choices for your physical body and mind; and, choose wisely from here on out.

Conclusion: How Long Will it Take?

This, finally, brings us to an end of this introduction to the Lightning Path. At this point, you know what the LP is, what it is about, where it originated from, what were/are some of the problems of development, and the principles upon which it is based. At this point I hope you have everything you need in order to make your decision. Of course, your decision is whether to step onto the Lightning Path and explore what it has to offer or find your own way back to full connection. Whatever you decide, know there are no hard feelings. It is entirely up to you what you want to do. If you want to look around inside the temple, fine. If you want to explore elsewhere, fine. If you want to give up all together, you can do that, too. It is totally up to you.

If you do decide to move forward on the LP, then an important final question to address is, how long will it take. At first glance, this might not seem like a relevant question, but it is. A lot of people think that enlightenment, awakening, salvation, the attainment of Nirvana, or whatever you want to call reconnection with The Fabric takes a long time, maybe even lifetimes. The Indigo Girls, a rock duo, wrote a song about it called "Galileo." In that song they lament, in cloying harmonies and saccharine riffs, the lifetimes it takes to "get it right" and reach the light. It is a popular idea in the popular consciousness that we are so fallen from grace and so low on the cosmic evolutionary scale that "it" (i.e. getting back to The Garden, redeeming ourselves, evolving to a higher level, etc.) must be very hard and must take a very long time. Academics share this view too, i.e. that it is difficult, challenging, hard, and takes a long time. I submitted a paper for review to a journal and was castigated once by a reviewer who told me that "In the traditions of the world of mystics, the mystical experience is attributed to such people who achieved a high degree of human maturity and were open to transcendence. *Often they passed demanding tests.*" He is saying what so many others say in one form or another. We are like Sisyphus struggling up the mountain only to be crushed again by the weight of a rock. It's a tough climb, and only the strong chosen few ever get to the top.

Isn't that right?

This is what we are told, isn't it?

When it comes to getting into heaven or attaining nirvana, this is what people think. I know it, because I see it all the time. But, it's just not true. We're not fallen angels; we're not karmic rejects; we're not evolving apes.[226] As we have seen in this short introduction to the Lightning Path, there are challenges, but these are hardly the moralistic, Sisyphean challenges that many see. Really, the question is not will you evolve or will you be redeemed; the question is, when will you realize who you really are and, in full realization, free yourself from The System and ascend to your true power and glory. The question, in short, is "How long will it take you to Realize?" The answer is, it depends on a lot of different things. It depends on the quality of the materials you choose to guide you home; it depends on the discipline and persistence you bring to the process; it depends on the courage and fortitude that you are able to muster; it depends on how supportive your home and social environments are; finally, it depends on the extent to which you process, understand, ground, and accept the truth. Because it depends on so many different things, it is difficult to predict even via informed professional assessment. The truth is you could have full God realization tomorrow, or it could take ten years. Realization could also come in a visionary instant, or it could gradually build up over the course of days or even months. I think it is possible to give an individual a general idea

---

[226] Well, that is not quite true. Our physical body has evolved, that's for sure. How exactly that happened and what, if anything, guided the process are still open to debate, but there can't be any doubt that our body evolved. But that's our body, and our brain. Our body, our brain, is just a vehicle, albeit a sophisticated one, for Consciousness, the Holy Spirit, Krishna, Allah, God, or whatever you want to call it. Our body is just one side of the proverbial coin.

of how long it might take them to achieve progress, but in order to do it properly you would have to know their family/childhood biography and their extant life conditions. You simply can't make accurate general statements.

Still, if your concern is moving forward as fast and as safely as possible, there are a few things I can say to help move things along.

First of all**, put the time in.** The more time you put in, the faster you will move. The more time you spend reading the materials, the more time you spend practicing the visualizations, the more time you spend thinking about the ideas and working on the stuff that needs to be worked on, the faster "it" (i.e. your shift, the shift) will happen. It is a straightforward relationship much like taking music lessons. If you put in fifteen minutes of practice a day, you will make fifteen minutes worth of forward progress each day. It will be progress, but it will be slow. On the other hand, if you put in three hours a day, you will improve much faster. The relationship is simple and no special talent or "gift" need be involved here. The more you commit, the more your self-discipline, the more you are able to reach out for help when you need it, the faster will be your progress indeed.

Second of all, **implement the changes you need to implement.** This is very important. *As you progress through the LP materials you are going to see more clearly the nature of reality around you.* As your reality comes into clearer focus, you will see that what surrounds you probably isn't as wonderful / supportive / beautiful as you may like to think. Many of us have been living a delusion (fueled by Hollywood and other Agents of Consciousness) of what the world is really like. As you progress you are probably going to see a lot more pain, anguish, toxicity, violence, and despair than you are comfortable with. It will be a challenge just facing this reality. However, if you stay long on the LP you are eventually going to hear the same message over and over again and that message is simply that *things must change.* If you want to make spiritual progress, it cannot be business as usual. If you want to make spiritual progress, much has to change. From the smallest daily activities to the widest social, political, and economic movements, things have to change, and they have to change fast. And the truth is, you are going to have to change them. Who else is there? If you don't change the things that need to be changed, if things remain status quo, then so do levels of consciousness in your body, and on this planet. And who wants that? So, if you want to make progress, prepare to make changes. If this freaks you out a bit, if you awaken and balk at the scope of the changes required, don't. We all start small, in our spaces and our own lives, and we all move forward from there. Start small. Start with what you can change and move forward from there. As we shall see in the next two LP units, even creating a safe cocoon for yourself amidst a sea of violence and abuse is an appropriate and important change.

Finally, in addition to admonishing you to put in the time and make the necessary changes I will say this, if you want to move forward quickly, **be discerning.** If you ask me, this planet's spirituality is really quite messed up. It is confused and confusing. Sometimes, as we'll learn, it is intentionally corrupted by those who would sacrifice the potential of human mystical connection to Consciousness for their own selfish, venal, purposes. I'm not pointing a finger in judgment here, I'm just saying, we've all been "sleeping at the wheel" so to speak. While sleeping we have messed things up quite a bit. If we want to move forward efficiently, we have to realize the spirituality of this planet is messy, confused, and corrupted, and we have to learn to think critically about how we approach that spirituality. This isn't to say that there isn't a lot of spiritual wisdom out there; it is just to say, it's a mixed bag. If you want to move forward, you have to sort it out. I know this is a big task, but the LP is designed to help with that. I have already mentioned the SpiritWiki, the LP Master Map, and the three LP *Rocket Guides*™ (i.e. *Rocket Scientists' Guide to Authentic Spirituality, Rocket Scientists' Guide to Money* and *the Economy,* and

Rocket Scientists' Guide to Discernment). All of these and more LP resources[227] are designed to increase your ability to understand, process, ground, and discern an authentic spirituality. There is a lot of material so you don't have to do it all at once; but, do keep in mind that there is more to this process than mystical connection and life changes. If you don't put in the effort to sort things out, you'll find your progress forward blocked by misconception, disorientation, and confusion.

In closing I just have to say this. Even though a lot of the weight for change falls directly onto your shoulders, keep in mind that everybody else needs to chip in as well. Despite what anybody says, *you can't do it alone.* Not even the richest most powerful person in the world can accomplish what needs to be done without the assistance and buy-in of everybody else. You will find that you are only going to be able to go so far, so fast, under your own steam. You have to understand, you are impacted by the spiritual and energetic conditions around you. These conditions can *limit* or *enhance.* If you live in negative and suppressive conditions, these conditions prevent forward movement. If you live in positive and aligned conditions, these conditions support and enhance forward movement. The important lesson here is that in the end *this is a collective process that depends on collective conditions.* If you think you are a spiritual island floating isolated in a sea of consciousness, you're wrong. *We are not islands in a sea of consciousness; we are the waves of a vast cosmic ocean.*

If you want to wrap your head around what I am saying here, think of it like this. Imagine you are in a swimming pool and the pool is filled with mud, sludge, gunk and garbage. In conditions like that, you are not going to be able to have a lot of fun. In fact, in conditions like that you will spend most of your time cleaning off the gunk that keeps settling back on your

---

[227] I think specifically here about my *Book of the Triumph of Spirit* series.

body. It is the same way with the spiritual life of this planet. You may want to awaken, activate, and ascend, but as long as everybody else around you remains mired in the gob and gunk of blindfolded existence, crystals, singing bowls, meditations, visualizations, and intent will only go so far. You will make some progress, but you will ultimately be dragged down, limited, and perhaps even choked by the crap around you. I'm not saying this to discourage you; this is just what we have to work with. Given these conditions, the only solution to the limitations caused by the dirty swimming pool is to *clean up the crap*. And don't do it for you and yours only. This entire planet must be cleaned up. *If we want to attain our full potential as manifested monads of Spirit, we are going to have to make this world a better place for everyone.* There is no choice. *We move forward to Connection together, or we do not move forward at all.* And if the thought of this overwhelms you, once again, calm down. You do not have to manifest major transformation in the next spiritual instant or alone and all by yourself. This is a collective process and while it might seem like an insurmountable challenge in this moment, it is not. Once the ball gets rolling the collective work of billions will make the cleanup work easy. Start with yourself and your local spaces and when that's done, when you and your local spaces are ready, you will find others will be ready as well. Join hands with those you meet and very soon you will find a global transformation of light, love, compassion, and divinity has already occurred, like magic, right before your eyes.

I am Michael Sharp.

Welcome home.

Organizing Your Workgroup

This book can be used for individual study or as a foundation for group work. This book is specifically designed to facilitate individual study *or* classroom based exploration. If you are interested in doing spiritual workgroups, you can easily manage the group using the tools and techniques provided here. My suggestion is that you get the group to read a single chapter before the group meets, and then when the group meets, the class can discuss the individual questions and key concepts.

If your workgroup or classroom is small, say less than eight people, you can discuss the questions and concepts as a whole. However, if your group is larger than eight, consider breaking up the larger group into smaller groups of no more than six people. Don't expect each group to deal with all the questions. Break the questions and concepts up and assign one or more (as necessary) to each individual or group.

The individual groups should pick a transcriber, someone who will write the group's thoughts down. The transcriber is responsible for accurately representing what the group is thinking.

The group also needs to pick a representative, i.e. one who will stand in front of the larger group or class and share the group's discussion. The representative can use the notes of the transcriber, or they can use their own notes so long as they are complete.

As a workgroup facilitator, your job is to walk amongst the groups, listen to what they are saying, and help move their discussion along. Contribute ideas and corrections as necessary. Pay attention to group dynamics. Are some monopolizing the conversation? Do some seem too shy to contribute? Address these issues with compassion and concern. The goal is to create workgroups where everybody is comfortable to speak. To do that you may have to be supportive and encouraging, and you may have to engage in a little psychotherapy.

When it comes to selecting a representative, encourage the group members to be thoughtful. First, individuals should volunteer. If more than one person expresses an interest in representing the group, *rotate* them. Encourage the group to discuss with the representatives what makes a good representative. As a start to the discussion, a good representative should be calm, will fairly represent all opinions, is a good speaker, and (most importantly) is capable of accepting criticism. Encourage the group to give the representatives *positive* feedback after each presentation. Criticism is acceptable if given with the intent to strengthen and uplift. Criticism intended to undermine and destroy has no place in a functioning spiritual workgroup (or any workgroup for that matter).

Note, bulk purchases of LP workbooks can be made at a 40% or higher discount at http://press.thelightningpath.com/path

Teaching Supports

This workbook comes with various teaching supports, like a twitter feed of ideas and quotes from the book, a Quizlet that allows you to easily study vocabulary and other LP concepts. For a complete list of available supports, and an overview of LP curriculum, see http://www.thelightningpath.com/fast-path/

Key Concepts

I have introduced and/or developed several key concepts and ideas in this book. Below you will find a list of these concepts. You will also find an index of these concepts at the back of the print version of this book. By now you should be familiar with these concepts.

- Abraham Maslow
- Agents of Consciousness
- Agents of Socialization
- Alignment
- Archetypes
- Authentic Spirituality
- Avatar
- Bodily Ego
- Church God / Science God
- Clearing Experience
- Connection
- Consciousness Quotient
- Disjuncture
- EPMO
- Exploration and Exposition Principles
- Fabric of Consciousness
- Glimmering/Glimpse
- Holy Grail
- Kingdom of God/Heaven/The Garden
- Lateral Ideology
- Nadir Experience /Zenith Experience
- New Energy
- New Energy Archetypes
- Noesis
- Old Energy
- Peaker / Non-Peaker
- Normal Consciousness
- Resident Monadic Self
- Right Action / Right Thought / Right Environment
- Self
- Signal Emotions
- Sin
- Spiritual Appliance

- Spiritual Ideology
- Stream of Consciousness
- Syncretism
- Synod of Hippo
- The Path
- The System
- The Word
- Toxic Socialization
- William James

Study Questions

Study questions are here for those wishing to do group study, for those seeking LP certification, or for those studying to be Lightning Path mentors. If you are a member of a spiritual study group, read the chapter and answer the questions either by yourself, or in group discussion. Share your thoughts and answers with the group. If you are studying to be a LP student, answer these questions and submit online. If you are not studying as an LP student, you may still find it useful to at least read and consider the questions. Like reading over the key concepts above, doing so will help orient you to the content and prime you to extract key concepts and ideas from the text.

The LP in a Nutshell

1. In your own words, describe the Lightning Path. What does it do and how does it do it. Name five things the LP does to encourage mystical connection. Name some obstacles to mystical connection?
2. What is Spiritual Emancipation? How is spiritual emancipation related to Connection? Why do we seek spiritual emancipation? Is spiritual emancipation something that you feel drawn to achieving? Share with the group.
3. Getting connected is a challenge, but staying connected even more so. Describe some things that prevent persistent connection. Do you see any of these things in your life? If so, spend some time thinking about it and describe the impact of one.

Doubt, Disbelief, and Disappointment

1. There are lots of reasons to doubt spirituality or reject a path like the LP, but there are reasons to give it a closer look. After reading this chapter, what are some of the reasons that convince you to take a closer look?
2. The LP shines a light. What are some of the things that the shining light of the LP can offer to those already happy

in a spiritual tradition?

3. In the textbook it says, the LP will not disappoint. Why will the LP not disappoint?
4. What does it mean to say the LP is the world's first open spiritual system? What are the benefits of an open and transparent spiritual system? Do you think all spiritual systems should be open?
5. What are the benefits of a "blended approach" to the spirituality and teachings of the LP? How might this blended approach appeal to the agnostic or atheist? Discuss.
6. What does it mean to pursue a balanced approach? Why is this important?

Reconnecting with The Fabric

1. What are some things that the text lists as "distraction" from the true goal of authentic spirituality, which is connection? Do you fill your life with these distractions? If so, what are you going to do about it?
2. If everybody has had a mystical experience at one time or another, why don't more people talk about mystical experience? Have you been silent about your mystical experiences? What fears/ideas have stilled your tongue?
3. What are the six things that the LP uses to facilitate authentic spiritual connection? Describe each briefly. What are the things that stand out the most for you? Share.
4. According to the text, the LP builds a support network. Why is this important? Can you think of other reasons besides those in the text, perhaps from your own mystical experiences, why support is important? Share.

Origins

1. This chapter discusses the origins of the Lightning Path in the mystical experiences and reflections of the author. The chapter also describes intellectual disjuncture, emotional resistance, and the fears that block forward

progress. Examine your own belief system. Are you atheist, agnostic, or one of the faithful? Why do you believe what you believe? Do you feel free to explore new spiritualities, or to be honest and open about it now? If not, why do you think that is? What are the fears, obstacles, and so on that block you up and prevent an open exploration? If you are working in a group, share your self-reflection with this group.

2. In this chapter many obstacles (mostly fears) are identified that might prevent an individual from "moving forward" on a spiritual pathway. List the fears, blockages, and issues that resonated the most with you. Write them down and think about them. From where do you think the obstacles arise? What can you do to overcome them? Share your thoughts with the group.

3. The Lightning Path is a blended path. It aspires to meld science and spirituality together into a logical, unified, and productive whole. List some of the benefits of this blended path as outlined in the workbook. Can you think of any more benefits not listed? Share.

Some Challenges

1. The workbook lists several challenges that we might face when making a mystical connection. List them on a piece of paper and describe them in your own words. Have you ever had a mystical connection experience? Can you relate to any of the challenges? Share with the group.

2. What does it mean to say that the Lightning Path is a totally new lump of clay? Why is a new lump of clay necessary? Be sure to discuss the significance of ideology. Also reflect on the presence of ideology in your own spiritual tradition.

3. What are the intellectual challenges to communicating about spirituality? Do you have trouble talking about spirituality with others? Why is that? Consider the damaged spiritual-intellectual fabric of this planet and the

challenge of syncretism in your answer.

4. Have you tried to discuss human spirituality with family, friends, colleagues, and/or co-workers? If so, how did that go? Did you experience resistance? What did you do about it? Share.

LP Principles

1. What is EPMO (a.k.a. Rocket Science)? What are the consequences of EPMO for a spiritual seeker? How does the LP combat EPMO?
2. The LP rejects all notions of hierarchy and privilege. List the things listed in the text (e.g., no racism, no judgment) that the LP rejects in this instance. Can you think of anything else that should be rejected as we reject hierarchy and privilege?
3. What is the difference between sex and gender? Is creating a world of gender difference necessarily a bad thing? Why or why not?
4. Outline and discuss the LP's political position vis a vis ethnicity and gender? Do you agree with this? Why or why not?
5. What does it mean to say that the LP strives for the truth and nothing but, no strings attached? Outline some of the details. Why do you think this is an important E&E principle?

How Long Will it Take?

1. What three things can you do to to ensure your awakening and activation process moves forward as fast and efficiently as possible.
2. The metaphor of the dirty swimming pool is meant to illustrate what important spiritual principle? How do you think this principle applies to your own life? Discuss.

About the Author

Michael Sharp is a Sociologist with a specialization in psychology, religion, occult studies, social inequality, scholarly communication, and critical theory. After a dramatic crown chakra opening caused him to question the materialist foundation of modern science, he began exploring the spiritual and mystical side of life. Recognizing early the presence of elitism and patriarchy in the world's religious and "secret" traditions, he began creating a new, open system of mysticism free of the opportunistic bias in "old energy" systems. The Lightning Path™ is the culmination of his research and work. Visit Michael at http://www.michaelsharp.org

About the Lightning Path

The Lightning Path (or simply LP for short) is an intellectual, emotional, psychological, and spiritual system of awakening and empowerment (a "mystery school" if you like, but without all the useless mystery) designed to help you get off the sinking ship of the old world and make "the shift" into an awakened, activated, and ascended state of existence. It is sophisticated, powerful, logical, grounded, rational, intellectually and metaphorically rigorous, politically sophisticated, empirically verifiable, authentic, effective, and accessible to everyone regardless of race, class, or gender. For more information visit http://www.thelightningpath.com

Index

Abraham Maslow, 11, 19, 21, 32, 50, 51, 71, 72
Agents of Consciousness, 27, 62
Agents of Socialization, 144
alignment, 28, 29, 30, 31, 48
archetypes, 11, 24, 26, 27, 31, 32, 85, 91, 142
authentic spirituality, 11, 17, 19, 38, 46, 48, 68, 71, 117, 136, 156
Avatar, 57, 58, 59
blocking emotions, 26
Bodily Ego, 10, 80, 100
Church God, 96, 97, 133
clearing experience, 26, 82
Connection, 10, 11, 12, 13, 16, 24, 26, 55, 66, 72, 94, 100, 118, 120, 128, 129, 149, 161, 163
connection blockage, 26
connection experience, 16, 18, 23, 38, 50, 53, 68, 71, 74, 128
connection pathologies, 122
connection pathology, 66
Consciousness Quotient, 30
disjuncture, 28, 29, 30, 31, 164
double-N mystic, 108
ego explosion, 121
Emancipation, 17, 18, 163
EPMO, 36, 137, 138, 139
Fabric of Consciousness, 10, 11, 17, 19, 21, 22, 23, 24, 32, 37, 50, 60, 64, 67, 71, 73, 77, 80, 121, 132, 140, 141, 145
   The Fabric, 10, 11, 12, 17, 18, 20, 21, 22, 24, 38, 43, 46, 47, 48, 50, 53, 54, 60, 64, 71, 72, 77, 82, 121, 122, 132, 136, 145, 149, 152
glimpse, 24, 48
Holy Grail, 12, 19, 47
ideological bleed, 135
Kingdom of God, 22
Kingdom of Heaven, 17, 55, 57, 64
lateral ideology, 110
nadir experience, 72
new energy, 91
noesis
   noetic, 39, 40, 82, 107, 108, 119, 120, 121
non-peakers, 50, 51
normal consciousness, 31, 34, 83, 84
old energy, 24, 27, 91, 114, 126, 149, 167
Path, 163
peakers, 50
Peter Berger, 41
physical unit, 25, 26, 27, 28, 29, 30, 32, 48, 55, 63, 64, 66, 69, 117, 143, 145
Ram Dass, 85, 111
Resident Monadic Self, 28
right action, 69
right environment, 69
right thought, 69
Science God, 97
Self, 18, 27, 28, 59, 60, 125, 138
signal emotions, 30
sin, 37, 109, 125, 126
spiritual appliance, 94
spiritual ego, 10, 29, 30, 128
spiritual ideology, 61, 63, 111, 112, 113, 114, 118
Stream of Consciousness, 81
Synod of Hippo, 115
The Garden, 22, 152
The Path, 31
The System, 18, 19, 27, 71, 111, 144, 153
The Word, 34
toxic socialization, 25, 26, 51, 61, 63, 64
William James, 11, 21, 65
zenith experience, 72

References

Alighieri, Dante. *The Divine Comedy*. Trans. Johnson, Henry. New Haven: Yale University Press, 1915.

Anon. "Edward Carpenter: Red, Green and Gay." *Socialism Today* 131 (2009).

Aurobindo, Sri. *The Mother*. Pondicherry: Sri Aurobido Trust, 2013.

Berger, Peter. *A Bleak Outlook Is Seen for Religion*. Vol. April 25: The New York Times, 1968.

---. *The Descularization of the World: Resurgent Religion and World Politics*. Grand Rapids MI: Eerdmans, 1999.

---. *The Sacred Canopy: Elements of a Sociological Theory of Religion*. New York: Anchor Books, 1969.

Blake, William. *The Portable Blake*. New York: Penguin, 1977.

Bock, Darrell L. *The Missing Gospels: Unearthing the Truth Behind Alternative Christianities*. Nashville, Tennessee: Thomas Nelson, 2006.

Boehme, J. *The Signature of All Things, with Other Writings*. London: J.M. Dent & Sons, 1912.

Bourque, Linda Brookover. "Social Correlates of Transcendental Experiences." *Sociological Analysis* 30 3 (1969): 151-63.

Bruce, Steve. *God Is Dead: Secularization in the West*. Oxford: Blackwell, 2002.

Bucke, R.M. *Cosmic Consciousness*. New York: E.P. Dutton, 2009/1929.

Carpenter, Edward. *The Art of Creation: Essays on the Self and Its Powers*. London: Georbe Allen & Unwin, 1921.

Clarke, Arthur C. *Childhood's End*. New York: Del Rey, 1987.

Cohn, Steven F., and Kyriacos C. Markides. "Religion and Spiritual Experience: Revisiting Key Assumptions in Sociology." *International Journal of Transpersonal Studies* 32 2 (2013): 34-41.

Cook, C. C. H. "Psychiatry and Mysticism." *Mental Health, Religion & Culture* 7 2 (2004): 149-63.

Cross, John of the. *The Living Flame of Love*. Trans. J, Ackerman. Kindle: Magisterium Press, 2015.

Dawkins, Richard. *The God Delusion*. New York: Mariner Books, 2006.

Decker, Ronald, Thierry Depaulis, and Michael Dummett. *A Wicked Pack of Cards: The Origins of the Occult Tarot*. New York: St Martin's Press, 1996.

Decker, Ronald, and Michael Dummett. *A History of the Occult Tarot, 1870-1970*. London: Duckworth, 2002.

Dobbelaere, Karel. "Trend Report: Secularization: A Multi-Dimensional Concept." *Current Sociology* 29 2 (1981): 3-153.

Dodds, E. R. *The Greeks and the Irrational*. Berkeley: University of California Press, 1951.

Dossey, Larry. "The Brain as Filter: On Removing the Stuffing from the Keyhole." *Explore: The Journal of Science and Healing* 8 6 (2012): 317-22.

Drazenovich, George, and Celia Kourie. "Mysticismand Mental Health: Acritical Dialogue." *Hervormde Teologiese Studies* 66 2 (2010): 1-8.

Dummett, Michael. *The Game of Tarot*. London: Duckwork, 1980.

Durkheim, Emile. *The Elementary Forms of Religious Life*. New York: Free Press, 1965 (1912).

Ehrman, Bart D. *Lost Scriptures*. New Yok: Oxford University Press, 2003.
---. *Misquoting Jesus: The Story Behind Who Changed the Bible and Why*. Harper One, 2007.
Eliade, M. *Shamanism: Archaic Techniques of Ecstasy*. New York: Pantheon Books, 1964.
Evans-Wents, W.Y. *The Tibetan Book of the Dead, or the after-Death Experiences of the Bardo Plane, According to Lama Kazi Dawa-Samdup's English Rendering [1927]*. London: Oxford University Press, 1960.
Freeman, A. "The Sense of Being Glared At: What Is It Like to Be a Heretic?" *Journal of Consciousness Studies* 12 6 (2005): 4-9.
Grof, Stanislav, and Christina Grof. *Spiritual Emergency: When Personal Transformation Becomes a Crises*. New York: Putnam, 1989.
Happold, F.C. *Mysticism: A Study and Anthology*. New York: Penguin Books, 1963.
Harmless, William. *Mystics*. New York: Oxford University Press, 2008.
Heriot-Maitland, Charles P. "Mysticism and Madness: Different Aspects of the Same Human Experience?" *Mental Health, Religion & Culture* 11 3 (2008): 301-25.
Hermanns, William. *Einstein and the Poet*. Boston: Branden Books, 1983.
Inge, Rev. W. R. *Mysticism in Religion*. New York: Hutchinson's University Library, 2005.
Jackson, Mike, and K.W.M. Fulford. "Spiritual Experience and Psychopathology." *Philosophy, Psychiatry, & Psychology* 4 1 (1997): 41-65.
Jahn, R., and B. Dunne. "Sensors, Filters, and the Source of Reality." *Filters and Reflections: Perspectives on Reality*. Eds. Jones, Z., et al. Princeton: ICRL Press, 2009. 3-4.
James, William. *The Varieties of Religious Experience: A Study of Human Nature*. New York: Penguin, 1982.
Jantzen, Grace M. *Power, Gender, and Christian Mysticism*. New York: Cambridge University Press, 1995.
Kelly, T.R. *A Testament of Devotion*. New York: Harper & Brothers, 1941.
Kuhn, Alvin Boyd. *Theosophy: A Modern Revival of Ancient Wisdom (Phd Thesis)*. Whitefish, Montana: Kessinger Publishing, 1930.
Luby, J., et al. "The Effects of Poverty on Childhood Brain Development: The Mediating Effect of Caregiving and Stressful Life Events." *JAMA Pediatrics* 167 12 (2013): 1135-42.
Marx, Karl. "The German Ideology." *The Marx-Engels Reader*. Ed. Tucker, R. New York: Norton, 1978.
Maslow, A. H. "The "Core-Religious" or "Transcendent" Experience." *The Highest State of Consciousness*. Ed. White, John. New York: Doubleday, 2012. 339-50.
---. "The Farther Reaches of Human Nature." *Journal of Transpersonal Psychology* 1 1 (1969): 1-9.
---. "Lessons from the Peak-Experiences." *Journal of Humanistic Psychology* 2 1 (1962): 9-18.
---. *Motivation and Personality (2nd Ed.)*. New York: Harper & Row, 1970.
---. *Religions, Values, and Peak-Experiences*. New York: Penguin, 1994.
---. *Towards a Psychology of Being (2nd Edition)*. New York: Van Nostrand Reinhold Company, 1968.
Maslow, A.H. *The Farther Reaches of Human Nature*. New York: Viking, 1971.
---. "A Theory of Human Motivation." *Psychological Review* 50 4 (1943): 370-96.
Mulkay, Michael J. "Norms and Ideology in Science." *Social Science Information* 15 4-5 (1976): 637-56.

Myers, F.W.H. "The Subliminal Consciousness." *Proc Soc Psychical Res* 7 (1892): 298-355.

Newberg, Andew, Eugene d'Aquile, and Vince Rause. *Why God Won't Go Away: Brain Science and the Biology of Belief*. Ed. York, New. New York: Ballantine Books, 2001.

Newberg, Andrew, and Mark Robert Waldman. *How God Changes Your Brain: Breakthrough Findings from a Leading Neuroscientist*. New York: Ballantine Books, 2009.

Otto, Rudolf. *The Idea of the Holy*. Oxford: Oxford University Press, 1917.

Parmar, Hitesh. *Paradise Lost and the Divine Comedy: A Comparative Study*. New Delhi: Sarup & Sons, 2002.

Pinchbeck, Daniel. *Breaking Open the Head: A Psychedelic Journey into the Heart of Contemporary Shamanism*. New York: Broadway Books, 2003.

Plato. *The Republic*. New York: Dover Publications, 2000.

Rowbotham, Sheila. *Edward Carpenter: A Life of Liberty and Love*. New York: Verso, 2008.

Sharp, Michael. *The Book of Life: Ascension and the Divine World Order*. St. Albert, AB: Lightning Path Press/Avatar Publications, 2003.

---. *The Book of Light: The Nature of God, the Structure of Consciousness, and the Universe within You*. Vol. one -air. 4 vols. St. Albert, Alberta: Lightning Path Press, 2006.

---. *The Book of Light: The Nature of God, the Structure of Consciousness, and the Universe within You*. Vol. two - water. 4 vols. St. Albert, Alberta: Lightning Path Press, Unpublished.

---. *The Book of Magic*. Vol. 1. 7 vols. St Albert, Alberta: Lightning Path Press, unpublished.

---. *The Book of the Triumph of Spirit: Halo/Sharp New Energy Archetypes*. St. Albert.

---. *The Book of the Triumph of Spirit: Master Key*. St Albert, Alberta: Lightning Path Press, Unpublished.

---. *The Book of Triumph of Spirit: Healing and Activating with the Halo/Sharp System*. St. Albert: Lightning Path Press, 2013.

---. "Daughters of Isis". St Albert, Alberta, 2003. Lightning Path Press2014. <http://www.michaelsharp.org/daughters-of-isis/>.

---. "Ego Explosion". Sturgeon County, 2014. *The Blog of Michael Sharp*. The Blog of Michael Sharp. <http://www.michaelsharp.org/ego-explosion/>.

---. *The Great Awakening: Concepts and Techniques for Successful Spiritual Practice*. St. Albert, Alberta, Canada: Lightning Path Press, 2007.

---. "I Am/We Are". St Albert, Alberta, 2003. Lightning Path Press2014. <http://www.michaelsharp.org/i-am-we-are/>.

---. *Lightning Path Book Two - Foundations* Lightning Path Lesson Series. Ed. Sharp, Michael. Vol. 2. St. Albert, Alberta: Lightning Path Press, 2013.

---. *Lightning Path Workbook Four - Foundations*. Lightning Path Workbook Series. Ed. Sharp, Michael. Vol. 4. St. Albert, Alberta: Lightning Path Press, Unpublished.

---. "Parable of the Room". 2003. Feb 27 2014. <http://www.michaelsharp.org/parable-of-the-room/>.

---. *The Rocket Scientists' Guide to Authentic Spirituality*. St. Albert, Alberta: Lightning Path Press, 2010.

---. *The Rocket Scientists' Guide to Money and the Economy: Accumulation and Debt*. St Albert, Alberta: Lightning Path Press., 2016.

---. "Shambhala Warriors". St Albert, Alberta, 2003. Lightning Path Press2014. <http://www.michaelsharp.org/shambhala-warriors/>.

---. *The Song of Creation: The Story of Genesis*. St. Albert: Lightning Path Press, 2006.

---. "Toxic Socialization". 2016. The SpiritWiki. January 15 2016. <http://www.thespiritwiki.com/Toxic_Socialization>.

Smith, H. *The Religions of Man*. New York: Harper & Row, 1958.

Sosteric, Mike. "Dangerous Memories: Slavery, Mysticism, and Transformation". Spirituality Studies, 2016. Unpublished Manuscript: Academia.edu. 7/20 2016. <https://www.academia.edu/25031557/Dangerous_memories_-_Slavery_mysticism_and_transformation>.

---. "Ding Dong the Alpha Male Is Dead." *The Socjourn* (2012).

---. "Gendered Activities, Gender Difference, Gender Exclusion." *The Socjourn* (2012).

---. "Mysticism, Consciousness, Death." *Journal of Consciousness Exploration and Research* 7 11 (2016): 1099-118.

---. "The Science of Ascension: Bodily Ego, Consciousness, Connection". 2016. <https://athabascau.academia.edu/DrS>.

---. *The Sociology of Mysticism*. ISA eSymposium for Sociology.

---. "A Sociology of Tarot." *Canadian Journal of Sociology* 39 3 (2014).

---. "Subjectivity and the Labour Process: A Case Study in the Food and Beverage Industry." *Work, Employment, and Society* 10 2 (1996).

---. "Toxic Socialization." *Socjourn* (2016).

Starr, Bernard. *Jesus Uncensored: Restoring the Authentic Jew*. OmniHouse Publishing, 2013.

Underhill, Evelyn. *Mysticism: A Study in the Nature and Development of Spiritual Consciousness*. New York: Dover Publications, 2002 (1911).

Vaughan-Lee, Llewellyn. *Catching the Thread: Sufism, Dreamwork & Jungian Psychology*. Inverness, CA: Golden Sufi Center, 1998.

Vergote, A. "Plying between Psychology and Mysticism." *Mysticism: A Variety of Psychological Perspectives*. Eds. Belzen, Jacob A and Antoon Geels. New York: Rodopi, 2003. 81-107.

Whoriskey, Peter. "As Drug Industry's Influence over Research Grows, So Does the Potential for Bias." *The Washington Post* 2012.

Wisse, Frederik. "The Apocryphon of John." *The Nag Hammadi Library*. New York: Harper Collins, 1990.

Yamane, David, and Megan Polzer. "Ways of Seeing Ecstasy in Modern Society: Experiential-Expressive and Cultural-Linguistic Views." *Sociology of Religion* 55 1 (1994): 1-25.

Yoshikawa, H., J. L. Aber, and W. R. Beardslee. "The Effects of Poverty on the Mental, Emotional, and Behavioral Health of Children and Youth: Implications for Prevention." *Am Psychol* 67 4 (2012): 272-84.

Zimmer, H. *Philosophies of India*. Princeton, NJ: University Press, 1951.